School's Out! The Definitive Guide to Leaving Teaching and Rebalancing Your Life

Phil Fletcher

Contents

Introduction

We all face crises in our lives, and in times of crisis we find it useful to reach out and find help and hope from others. For many teachers, use of the word "crisis" is not an overstatement when it comes to describing where they have found themselves in their professional lives.

Teaching is a demanding profession to put it mildly. Many teachers find themselves in very difficult circumstances in their schools or colleges and for the first time start to ask themselves the question: is it time to move on? I found myself in this predicament and I felt lost. There were so many questions I had which I just didn't know how to answer. How should I decide whether to leave or whether to stay? What else could I do? Am I too old to start to train to do something else? Would I be able to make as much money as I do now? How would I pay my mortgage? What is the jobs market outside of teaching even like these days?

I found it hard to find answers to these very specific questions. To whom should I turn? Friends and family were certainly supportive and lent me a sympathetic ear but they weren't teachers. They didn't know about the nitty gritty of the day to day life of teachers and couldn't tell me the first thing about the likely job prospects for a teacher who wanted to leave the classroom. Similarly, those teacher friends who I told of my uncertainties were supportive too. But they didn't know about leaving teaching – they were still teachers. What's more, I didn't want to tell everyone at school that I was thinking of leaving. Teachers don't want word to spread that they're thinking of bailing out. Won't the headteacher think that you're being disloyal? Won't your colleagues think that you're leaving because you "can't cut it"? And won't your pupils start to take advantage if they think you're on your way out?

Teaching has the potential to be the most rewarding and fulfilling of all careers and when things go well one can experience an unparalleled sense of gratification. The other side of the coin is that when things take a turn for the worse, the feelings of despair and despondency are also unparalleled. When one feels like one is losing one's spark, when one feels like one is burning out, when one has lost that certain passion for one's subject, when one has lost discipline in their classroom… in these circumstances one can find oneself in a very dark place indeed. I have horrible memories of a time when I would arrive home in the evenings feeling completely exhausted, depleted and demoralised. The questions listed above swirled around in my head and I wondered whether there would ever be an end to this hell.

When I found myself in this situation, one of the things which I found most useful and encouraging was to visit the forums on the Times Educational Supplement website and read some of the stories there of teachers who had also found themselves in stickysituations. There were stories of teachers being bullied by management, stories of teachers who had lost control of their classes, stories of teachers being put through disciplinary procedures and in the most extreme cases there were teachers who were literally on the verge of suicide crying out for help.

Perhaps my motivation to read these stories was that of a strange sense of Schadenfreude, but this wasn't the only motivation. For alongside these tales of woe were uplifting tales of teachers who had "escaped".

"Escape" seems like a strange choice of verb to describe the process of leaving one job and going to another, something which is in fact an extremely common occurrence and something most of us typically go through multiple times during our lifetimes. However anyone who has been teaching for any length of time will know that it is often the most appropriate word to use. At times, especially when one is considering leaving, teaching can seem like some kind of strange cult. Yes – you can leave in theory, but according to your contract there are only three dates each year on which you can be legally permitted to leave. This means there are times when you may have to give as much as six months' notice if you want to leave. The ever increasing pay scale at times seems like it has been designed to trap you – by the time you have been teaching for a few years, you are almost certainly going to have to take a pay cut if you leave so you had better start contemplating some serious adjustments to your lifestyle. And surely you're not going to turn your back on everything you've worked so hard towards? There's all the training you've been through – that university course you took at a cost of thousands of pounds. There's all the time you spent developing those wonderful resources and schemes of work. And how embarrassing it will be to admit to your friends, family and colleagues that you're leaving! You'll look like a complete failure!

But for many people, "escape" is not only the right word but the right decision too. Having taken the plunge myself, I've never looked back and never been happier. The time during which I took that decision and worked towards finding an alternative however was one of the toughest periods of my life. I've written this book to try and help others through what can be an excruciatingly difficult phase of their professional lives.

This is a book written *by* a (former) teacher *for* teachers. I hope that it will serve two purposes. The first purpose is to help you decide *whether* you should leave the teaching profession. Just because I have left and it has turned out to be the correct decision for me, this does not necessarily mean that this is also the correct decision for you too. I want you to be able to arrive at your decision *rationally* by taking a dispassionate look at your life and values and deciding which course of action is likely to best help your reach your values, goals and ambitions in life.

The second purpose of this book is to help those who have decided that they would like to leave to make a transition to a life outside of teaching. Such a move is a difficult and daunting process to go through. It *could,* as so many people tell me, be the best move you ever make in your life, but only if you get it right.

I should perhaps deal with a potential criticism of this book right at the outset. Isn't it unethical to write a book encouraging teachers to leave the profession when our education system is stretched enough as it is and there is already a shortage of teachers? My first response to this is, as I said above, this is not a book that is encouraging teachers to leave. Rather, it is a book which is encouraging teachers to make the correct decision for themselves and indeed their loved ones. This may involve leaving teaching, it may involve staying or it may involve staying and making some kind of adjustment such as going part time or moving to a different educational setting.

Secondly, there *is* in fact a part of me that thinks that what is needed is for a significant number of teachers to leave the profession so that the Government will wake up and realise that the working conditions of teachers need to be dramatically improved. Unfortunately, the working conditions for teachers seem to have become progressively worse over the last few years. The Government has been very clever in creating such a plurality of different schools (local authority schools, schools in academy chains, standalone academies etc.) that it is very difficult to come up with one uniform agreement for teachers' working conditions in all instances.

All of this perhaps explains why in an industry where practitioners must have not just an undergraduate degree but a postgraduate qualification too the starting salary is £22,244[1] for an average working week of 55.7 hours[2] (this is the figure for secondary teachers, for primary it rises to 59.3 hours). This compares to the average salary of a London Underground tube driver who starts on a salary of £49,673 for a 36 hour working week.[3]

It could sadly be the case that the only way that the situation with respect to teachers' workload will improve is if more teachers start to vote with their feet. I am not suggesting for one second that successful, happy teachers should leave their jobs and become martyrs just to make a point. But what I am saying is that there is a potential win-win situation to engineer here. I believe that there are many unhappy teachers who could find more happiness in their lives if they found a different profession. Many of these teachers do not leave their jobs as they're not quite brave enough to take the plunge or in many cases they don't even contemplate such a move in the first place. The Government is taking full advantage of this inertia, but with one recent survey suggesting that 43% of the profession are planning on leaving in the next five years[4], it's possible that teachers may end up calling their bluff. This could of course cause some unwelcome disruption to pupil learning in the short term. However, pupils' interests are best served in the longer term if they are taught by motivated and enthusiastic teachers as opposed to exhausted and demoralised ones.

I should wrap up this introduction by expressing a debt of gratitude to those posters on the aforementioned Times Educational Supplement forums from whom I found inspiration during difficult times. Now that I have myself escaped, I take every opportunity to support those in need of assistance on these forums. After addressing multiple posts on these forums to frustrated career-changers I became frustrated myself by the fact that I could never communicate all that I wanted to communicate with these teachers in a short forum post. If only there were some way I could present all of what I had learned from my own career change to those who may stand to benefit from it? That is what this short book is.

If you find this book useful, please do follow me on Facebook where I intend to post updates and job finding tips. Also, I'd love it for you to get in touch and share your story with me, which you can do either on Facebook or email.

facebook.com/schoolsoutphilfletcher
contact.schoolsout.book@gmail.com

1. What's At Stake?

I suspect you've heard many times before Lao Tzu's adage that "a journey of a thousand miles begins with a single step". It is very useful to view a move out of teaching as a journey. A successful move out of the classroom is not something that one can achieve overnight. Even a retirement from teaching takes a little planning, and even if you win the lottery it would be rather irresponsible to simply walk out without serving your (potentially quite lengthy) notice period.

Should you make the decision to go, leaving teaching should become a *project* which is worked at over time. The good news is that "one thousand miles" is likely to be overstating it when it comes to giving an idea of the length of your journey. In my case, the length of time which elapsed from when I decided I was leaving to when I started in my new role outside of teaching was approximately five months, although I consider myself lucky in achieving this time frame and the typical time frame is perhaps slightly longer than this. The question I would like to answer initially is this however: what *is* the first step when it comes to leaving teaching? Is the first step speaking to your headteacher and telling them that you're unhappy? Is the first step browsing for new jobs on the internet? Is it handing in your notice at your current school and registering with a supply agency?

No – it isn't any of these things. You may be expecting me to say that the first step is *deciding* that you do in fact want to leave. But even this isn't strictly true. The true first step on the way out is merely *contemplating* leaving. It's in seeing that leaving is in fact a real and distinct possibility. One must not deny the existence or the significance of this step. Perhaps one of the most common regrets of those who leave teaching is not that they have left but that they didn't leave sooner. Any why didn't they leave sooner? They may never have even contemplated such a course of action.

This is a predicament I found myself in for many years. I believe that one of the main reasons that people find themselves in this situation is because teaching is something which is seen as a *career* as opposed to just a job. To my mind, a career is something which you typically do for your whole life, as opposed to a job which is something you do to pull in a bit of money until you get bored with it, at which point you will move on to your next job. Whilst thousands if not millions of workers across the land fantasise daily about leaving their dull "jobs", far fewer workers plan on ditching their "careers".

Few people enter teaching with the plan of then leaving a few years down the line (there is a possible exception here when it comes to initiatives such as Teach First). It's a little like entering a marriage – one knows in the back of one's mind that there is in theory the option to end it, but doing so is never Plan A. Young teachers fresh out of university enter the profession filled with idealism and hope. They want to transform young people's life chances. They want to become respected pillars of their local communities. Who knows, maybe they could even become a headteacher one day? These kinds of ambitions take decades to fulfil. Slightly older entrants to the profession may join teaching after working their way through a series of unfulfilling jobs. They qualify as teachers with the excitement of having now finally found a rewarding and fulfilling career. The days of an endless string of dead end jobs are finally behind them and they can now settle down in to an engaging career which will take them through to their retirement.

However, like a marriage, sometimes with teaching you have to accept that although you went in with the best of intentions, things simply aren't working out the way you had planned. Since teachers don't plan on quitting when they start out in the profession, often it takes an awful lot to get teachers to start contemplating alternatives. But everyone has their own personal tipping point and after several months or even years of pressure, stress and unhappiness, finally at long last that question pops inside the teacher's head: "is it time to call it a day?" Sadly, just as there are those who never seem to even consider leaving a difficult relationship, there are also those who never even reach this first step of seriously considering leaving. Of course, if you're a happy, fulfilled and successful teacher then why would you consider leaving? But if we're being honest with ourselves, we all have met teachers who seem to be always stressed, always unhappy, always doing nothing else other than counting down to that next half term break. We all know teachers who have been persisting in their jobs for decades despite not appearing to be particularly effective in them. The state of these teachers, many of whom take their denial right through to their retirement, is a sorry one indeed. The main purpose of this book is to try and prevent the grimmest of all possible outcomes – getting to the end of a misspent and unhappy career and realising that you've made a terrible mistake.

Therefore, contemplating alternatives, unless you're always super happy and fulfilled, is an important process for us all to go through. But there is an important piece of good news for you –

you're already reading this book. It seems highly unlikely that you would be doing so had you not contemplated leaving already. You've already taken an extremely important first step.

As I made clear in the introduction, this is not a book that is preaching to people that they ought to leave the teaching profession. This would be reckless, as such a decision is not necessarily going to be the right one for all readers. I remember when I was trying to make this decision myself I would speak to friends, colleagues and family and ask them for their advice. Many of them said to me "Phil, in the end this is a decision which only you can make yourself." What use was that?! When you're faced with a difficult dilemma, this is not what you want to hear. But just because it's not what you want to hear, that doesn't mean it isn't true. Life's big decisions are rarely simple or straight forward. My friends were right – you do have to make this decision yourself, but *how* do you do it? In the end, I made my decision the only way I knew how – *rationally* and *dispassionately*.

A rational decision about whether to leave teaching has to be taken by first thinking about what your goals, ambitions and values are in life. This is precisely why others can't make the decision for you – their goals, ambitions and values are likely to be different to yours. You should then go through a process of considering all the advantages and disadvantages of your current career and consider how these sit with your goals, ambitions and values. Then (perhaps after a little research) you consider the potential advantages and disadvantages of an alternative career and you should think too about how these sit with your goals, ambitions and values. You should then find yourself in a position where, difficult though it may be, you can weigh up alternatives and decide on which course of action is going to lead to maximum fulfilment and happiness.

Before I go in to more detail about the process of making a decision, I should perhaps talk a little more about the nature of the decision itself. First of all, I want you to realise that this decision is an extremely important one. Making this decision ought to take high priority in your life. If you're in a tricky spot right now career wise and are unhappy at work, it is possible that one of the causes of this is that in the past you perhaps didn't spend quite as much time thinking about the suitability of your career choices as you could have done. I know this is certainly true in my own case, but I think actually that we can all be forgiven for this. As teachers ourselves we all know that the quality of careers guidance which young people receive is often quite poor. Even if it weren't, many of us will still have found ourselves making some of our most important career decisions during the confusion of adolescence, a time when we're still struggling to understand ourselves and have an awful lot on our minds besides career choices.

So if previous career decisions haven't been quite as well researched as they might have been, buck this trend right now in thinking about your future choices. Taking some all-important time to reconsider career plans when you're a little older and understand yourself better is a very wise thing to do. Repeating the mistakes of the past isn't.

Secondly, I want you to realise that all decisions in life, especially big ones, carry an element of risk. Nobody can pull out a crystal ball and tell you which course of action will bring you the most happiness in future. Even if they could, this would serve to take much of the fun out of life! Suppose that, after much careful thought and consideration, you make an informed decision to leave teaching and pursue another profession which you have carefully researched and have decided is much more suitable for you. Suppose as well that despite all of your careful planning, your new career goes belly up and you end up rueing the decision that you made. Such is life! We have to accept that these things can happen, whilst realising at the same time that such misfortunes are not the end of the world and we can still come bouncing back from them. We must remember that with nothing ventured there is nothing gained. Eliminating risk entirely from life is not possible and those who attempt to do so often end up living the blandest lives of all.

Another thing I would like to point out on the subject of decisions and risk is that it's important to remember that *a decision not to act is just as significant as a decision to act*. You may think that the safest bet is likely to be staying in your existing career. Not handing in your notice, not leaving your job, not finding another career – all these things don't seem like decisions, they don't seem like bold or risky moves. Yet in reality they are. The decision to stay in your existing job is exactly that. It's a decision which is actively made and it is made simultaneously with the decision *not* to pursue another career and try something else. As with all decisions, this decision carries risk too. As I mentioned earlier, possibly the worse of all scenarios is to get to the end of your career and worry that your time has been misspent. We mustn't forget that when it comes to regrets we often regret much more bitterly those things that we didn't do as opposed to those thinks that we did do.

Finally, I think it's extremely important that you are able to keep your decision in perspective. This doesn't have to contradict my previous advice that this in an important decision which should take a high priority. If you become too bogged down by your deliberations and begin to find the very process of making your decision a source of stress in itself then you risk losing your ability to make your decision rationally and dispassionately. Making your decision a source of stress itself is especially foolish if you're already experiencing stress from your teaching job. Any additional stress is absolutely the last thing you need! How can you find a healthy perspective? I would actually advice that a good start is to begin seeing teaching more as a job as opposed to a career.

I said earlier that teachers do tend to view their work as a career rather than a job. This is partly what contributes to seeing the process of leaving as such a frightening one. But here is some food for thought: yes, you have to achieve a postgraduate qualification to become a qualified teacher, but that process only takes about ten months. Is that such a long amount of time in the grand scheme of things? Sure, the course costs thousands of pounds, but didn't you get thousands of pounds in bursaries too? There are plenty of occupations which aren't considered careers where it takes several months to train. Leaving teaching is no small decision but certainly wouldn't be as momentous a decision as leaving medicine, for example, where one has to train for at least five years to qualify. When you start to see teaching as more of a job and less of a career, it helps to take some of the weight out of the decision to potentially leave in a way which I think is actually quite healthy. Changing jobs is not at all unusual. I'd be very surprised if you couldn't name at least one of your friends who has changed their job recently. Even if we limit it to teaching, 50,140 teachers left their jobs in the 2015-2016 academic year and only 22% of these were retiring.[5]

Another way to try to maintain a healthy sense of perspective it to remind yourself that very few decisions in life are completely irreversible. Let's say you do leave teaching and it doesn't work out. Couldn't you always go back? No one can take your teaching qualification away from you, nor can they take away the years of teaching experience which will forever remain on your CV. I should concede that returning to the exact same school isn't always practical or possible and if you have worked hard to get yourself in to what you consider to be the right kind of school (whether that's an independent school, a grammar school or a particularly strong state comprehensive school) then you perhaps need to spend some additional time thinking about how you might feel about working somewhere very different. Nevertheless, thanks to a combination of low teacher retention rates and a continuing rise in pupil numbers, teaching is likely to remain a buyer's market for jobs (especially for those in shortage subjects). Even as things stand today, the Government already actively campaigns to get those who have left the profession back in to the classroom.[6]

I hope that in this chapter I have helped you to explore the nature of the decision that you are about to make. I want you to see that the stakes are high, but nonetheless you need to maintain a healthy sense of perspective too. We now move on to the most important part of the process – making your decision!

2. How to Make Your Decision

This is by far the most important chapter in this book, during which I hope to guide you through the process of making your decision. What then are you deciding exactly? Most likely you are trying to answer the rather simple question "should I leave the teaching profession?" As I said in the previous section, this is not a binary choice. As I see it, there are really three options. Option 1 is the status quo, you stay working as a teacher and things remain exactly as they are. Option 2 is to continue teaching but to make some kind of significant adjustment which could considerably change the nature of your working experience. Examples of this would be to start working part time, to move from the state to the independent sector, to step down from a position of responsibility or to move to a school which is considerably different to the one you are currently working at. Option 3 is to leave the teaching profession entirely. Unless you can afford to take a career break or are independently wealthy, this third option will most likely involve you searching for and securing employment in a new industry.

If you opt for option 1, then this could be the last chapter of this book which you need to read. Since you have taken the trouble to purchase this particular book, I suspect that there is a fair chance that your life could be in somewhat improved by taking either options 2 or 3. Having said that, option 1 is still worth some serious consideration. There is a big difference between, on the one hand, staying in your teaching job because you have weighed everything up and have genuinely decided that this is the best path for you, and on the other hand staying because you can't be bothered to consider any alternatives and don't want to put in the effort. If staying in teaching is the right decision for you then I urge you to take that decision, but please make sure that it is a decision and not just laziness. What's more, if you do make the decision to stay, settle on that decision for at least a year or two, at which point you may consider a re-evaluation of your choice. The absolute worst thing you can do is to spend years dilly dallying about leaving but never making a firm decision one way or another. This is something you must try to avoid – take a firm, informed decision and see it through by having the courage of your own convictions.

But hang on a moment, you might think. People reading this book are clearly dissatisfied with their current job to at least some extent. Am I really suggesting that people should continue with jobs that they don't like? Well, what I'm suggesting is that readers rationally make the optimal decision for their own circumstances. We have to accept that *no job is perfect*. There are no employers who are in the business of paying people simply to have fun. There are also very few workers out there who enjoy everything about their job all of the time. Stress, pressure, long hours, poor management… teaching does not have a monopoly on all of these things. Making a rational decision involves weighing up the pros and cons of teaching against possible alternatives.

If you go for either options 2 or 3 then you should continue reading after this chapter. Later chapters will offer practical tips on how you can make either a career adjustment or a complete career change. First though, we need to get on with working out which one of options 1, 2 or 3 is for you. What follows is not some sort of magic formula which will generate an answer for you. Rather, I offer a series of suggestions which I hope will eventually enable you to answer the question for yourself. The techniques below were extremely useful to me in helping to make my own decision. I hope you find them useful too.

Tip 1: Seek advice from friends, family and colleagues

I've put this particular tip first in my list for a good reason. If you're going through a tough time at work, then you may be in need of not just practical support to help you think through your future options but also a little emotional support too. As well as needing a bit of advice on what direction you could potentially take with your career, what you may also need is a shoulder to cry on and someone who can help you to let off a bit of steam. This is why seeking assistance from those who you are closest to is a very good place to start.

You may remember earlier I mentioned that it was a source of personal frustration to me that when I reached out to friends for help with my career dilemma many of them simply said "In then end Phil, this is a decision only you can make yourself." As I pointed out, this is very true. If you get this response, first of all be grateful that you have such wise friends. But second of all, you could probe these friends a little and ask if they can give you something a little more tangible to work with. Not all of your friends and loved ones however will give this answer so ask around and you will hear a range of interesting perspectives. The best people to ask for advice about anything are those who have known you the longest. Whilst nobody knows you better than yourself, it always fascinates me how those who have known me a long time are able to point out things about me which I had barely detected. By speaking to people you have known for a long time, you will most likely also be talking to people who knew you before you were a teacher. This is key. These people will be able to see whether you have changed in any way, for better or for worse, since you first entered the classroom. Personal change can take place so gradually that we barely detect it. When we're children and growing in height we never seem to notice this growth ourselves. We only seem to realise when we pay Aunty a visit and she declares "gosh haven't you grown!" Your friends may point out to you that you seem happier now, they may say that it seems like for the first time you seem to have a job you enjoy and sometimes they even get a little irritated as they can't shut you up about your career! On the other hand, they may observe that recently you always seem to look tired, drained or even exhausted. They may gently complain that they very rarely get the chance to socialise with you anymore and that their social invitations are almost always declined, with a busy evening of marking usually being cited as the reason. Whatever their testimony may be, listen very carefully and if several different people are providing the same commentary independently of one another then this really ought to make you think.

In my own conversations with friends and family I managed to solicit a range of different opinion about what I should do next. What struck me as interesting was the fact that nobody said to me anything along the lines of "What? You'd be *mad* to leave!

You've invested a hell of a lot of time and effort in to this, why on earth would you turn your back on it?!" Instead opinions seemed to range from "well it is a decision you need to take very carefully" to "look if you're feeling unhappy just get out mate. Life's too short." Another good piece of advice is to imagine that a friend came to you with exactly the same problem that you are having. What advice would you give them in that situation? I think there's a good chance you would say something along the lines of "Whatever you do don't allow yourself to be unhappy for any length of time. You only live once you know." Why is it that we tend to dish out platitudes like this? Probably because deep down we genuinely believe that they are true. But whilst we are quick to dish out advice like this to others, all too often we're not brave enough to put it in to practice ourselves.

If you know or have heard of someone who has taken the plunge and left teaching themselves, they could offer you a gold mine of useful information. Seek them out at all costs, even if it means an awkward Facebook message to someone you've neither spoken to nor seen for the past three and a half years. Online forums, such as the Times Educational Supplement forum can also be great places to go to for anonymous help and support. When it came to discussing my potential exit with my own colleagues, I chose to restrict this to a small group of my most trusted colleagues to confide in rather than throwing the subject out there for discussion at one of our whole school staff meetings. I also decided not to discuss my feelings with my headteacher until I had both decided I was leaving and found another job I wanted to apply for. These were very much personal choices and in hindsight I consider them to be wise ones.

Tip 2: Make a list of what you like and dislike

This is one of the first things I did when I was trying to make my own decision. You can't beat a good old fashioned list like this and they're great tools for helping to make any difficult decision, not just career dilemmas. Divide your page in to two columns and get writing. Spend a bit of time on this. If you've been teaching for a number of years now, there must be plenty of things you like about teaching. Why else would you have done it for so long? However, since you're reading this book, I suspect there are all too many things you dislike too.

When reflecting upon your finished list, remember that it is certainly not a case of counting up the quantity of entries in each column. Different entries in your list will carry a different weight. "I get the thrill of working with young people and helping them to achieve their potential" in the like column is unlikely to be completely counter-balanced by "I have to give up five evenings a year for parents' evenings" in the dislike column. One possibility would be to try giving each of your entries some kind of numerical weighting. Having said that, big decisions such as the one you're working on can rarely be made through an appeal to simple arithmetic. Once you've finished your list, you might use it to help you answer a very simple question: how much would you say you enjoy your job on a scale of 1 to 10? I believe this question is very powerful in helping you to think about whether it's time for a change. You must of course remember that very few people if any would give their job 10 out of 10, but at the same time I suspect that there are very few who would give their job a 4 or below either. If you find that your score is somewhere within the lower echelons of the 1 to 10 range, this could serve as an important wake up call.

Keep your list somewhere safe as most likely new ideas (both positive and negative) will pop in to your head throughout the course of the following week. Write these down as soon as you think of them or else you will forget!

Tip 3: Identify your life goals, ambitions and values

This is the part where you need to start getting a little bit philosophical. Compiling your list of likes and dislikes is all very well and good but as I said, the issue is the weighting which is assigned to each entry in your list. To decide on an appropriate way of weighting each entry, you need to take a little time to think about exactly what your goals, ambitions and values are in life. Only then can you start to decide which side of your metaphorical scales is the heaviest.

When life is running smoothly, many of us do not feel the need to spend a great deal of time thinking explicitly about what our values are. In times of crisis, and a career crisis is a perfect example, we need to turn to our values to help us make the tough decisions which will see us through. Some of us find our values through religion, others will say they rely simply on "common sense". Some may not be religious but may still have some guiding philosophy in their life which helps them, even if they couldn't pin that philosophy down exactly. But what are we really talking about when we talk about values? Values are things which exist in a hierarchy. We all, for example, value money. No one in their right mind would turn down a £1 million lottery cheque if it was offered to them. Similarly, we all value free time to spend pursuing hobbies and interests. Who doesn't want that? The question is what happens if there were a conflict between the two? Which is more important to you – money or free time?

Thinking about one's values therefore involves thinking about how important one thing is to you relative to other things. Here's a quick and simple exercise to help you think about your own personal set of values. Below is a list of things which we all tend to value and consider important. I've tried to choose things particularly relevant to career choices. Take a piece of scrap paper and order the following from least important at the bottom to most important at the top. By doing so, you've just created your own hierarchy of values.

Spending time with my partner
My own personal happiness
Having lots of free time
Pursuing hobbies and interests
Having a job where I can work reasonable hours
Helping others
Money
Independence
Job security
Having a job I find enjoyable
Mental well-being
Spending time with my children
Professional respect and prestige
The admiration of my friends, family and colleagues
Doing a job which I think is ethical
Spending time with friends
Time to party and have fun
Leaving a legacy

Obviously, there is no right or wrong answer here, but I hope that you'll find your list of likes and dislikes alongside your list of values to be useful tools in helping you to make a decision.

You should remember too that values can and indeed do change throughout the course of a lifetime. Your values could be different now from what they were when you decided you wanted to be a teacher. There's every chance too that ten years down the line your values will be different again from what they are now. But it is precisely because our values change that sometimes our careers need to change too if we are to continue to be true to ourselves.

Tip 4: Ask yourself why you became a teacher

For me, this one was the clincher. It was in asking and answering this question that I had something of an epiphany and decided I was going to leave teaching behind me.

Different teachers go in to teaching for different reasons and I think it's important that you understand in your own mind what your own reason was. For me, I thought that teaching would be enjoyable. When comparing teaching to the alternatives I thought that being in a classroom full of kids would be an awful lot more interesting than sitting in an office all day crunching numbers using a spreadsheet. In many ways this is true. But once I had decided upon what my reason was for starting out, I then asked myself the next question: "So Phil, *do* you find your job enjoyable?"

I still remember the moment when I answered this question. I was sitting in the very same chair that I am sitting in now, writing this book. The answer dawned on me suddenly...

"Ninety percent of the time... no, I don't enjoy my job."

I realised that I wasn't enjoying almost all of my lessons. I wasn't enjoying the planning, I wasn't enjoying the marking.

What exactly was I enjoying? It hadn't necessarily always been like that. I remembered that there was a time when I did enjoy it. I even remember saying to myself that I would still continue with my job even if the day came when I didn't need to financially. But for one reason or another, this day had gone and if I was being honest with myself I was only getting out of bed and going in to work each morning so that I could earn the money to pay my mortgage. This realisation in some senses was a moment of disappointment but also a moment of relief too. Now my decision had been made.

There was in my case probably a secondary reason for entering the teaching profession. I saw it as an opportunity for self-development and I thought it would give me the chance to sharpen certain skills which would be useful in both my professional and personal lives. To an extent, I felt like I had achieved this and I wasn't really sure how much further teaching could take me with this goal.

Of course, your reasons may be very different from mine. Broadly speaking, I think that most reasons for entering teaching can be divided in to two categories: self-interested reasons and altruistic reasons. My two reasons were self-interested ones. It was about what *I* could get out of it. Other self-interested reasons would be going in to teaching for the long holidays, or because it offers a better salary than what one is able to find elsewhere. It's tempting to think that these self-interested reasons are the wrong reasons to go in to teaching, but they don't have to be. I was hoping to find myself in a win-win scenario. Yes, I would enjoy teaching and that was my motivation for going in. But surely my pupils would enjoy my lessons too, so long as I was a good teacher? I get the enjoyment and a pay cheque and they get an education. Everyone's a winner.

However, some people who go in to teaching for self-interested reasons will fall in to the trap of not realising just how much passion and dedication is required to succeed in teaching. You've got to really want to do it and you've got to really want to be there, every day! Children are very skilled in detecting when teachers are not passionate about what they're doing and once this happens these children are very quick to lose respect for the adult in front of them.

The more altruistic reasons for entering teaching are things like "I want to improve young people's life chances", "I want to inspire young people to have the same love of history that I have" or "I want help young people from deprived backgrounds to overcome their disadvantages and succeed in life." These reasons sound a lot more noble than the self-interested reasons but often these teachers can still fall in to their own traps. Altruistic teachers are often more likely to find themselves in tougher school settings – often because they have quite deliberately chosen to work with some of the most disadvantaged children. They therefore may end up having a tougher time than their more self-interested counterparts who have no qualms at all about working in an independent school or a grammar school whilst doing a heavy dose of private tutoring in the evenings too.

Those who entered the profession for more altruistic reasons than I did can still put themselves through the same test that I put myself through. If your main reason for entering the classroom was to "make a difference" then try (I know this can be hard) to ask yourself the question *"am* I making a difference?" Answer this question as candidly as you can. Of course, *every* teacher does make a difference, but are you making as much of a difference as you had once envisaged you would? If every day is a battle against bad behaviour and support from management is lacking, then it is possible that actually little difference is being made despite your Herculean efforts. If you do come to think this, do not beat yourself up about it. The problem is not you, it's the system. You could try to change and influence the system from within, and I would salute you for doing this. But please accept that there is a distinct possibility that you could get to the end of a career lasting decades and in fact the system has changed very little, or even gotten worse. You have to be able to live with this as a possible outcome.

The point I am making in this section is that if you feel like you may have gone in to teaching for the wrong reasons, or if you feel that teaching is simply not living up to what you expected it to be and never will, then you may wish to consider leaving. I'd like to mention at this stage too one reason for entering teaching which I think is almost always a bad one. I remember asking someone once why he went in to teaching and he said "I guess it's because I just enjoyed my own school days so much myself." Trying to relive your own childhood vicariously through the lives of the pupils you are teaching is surely always a mistake. Similarly, trying to combat loneliness or unhappiness in your adult life through some sort of pseudo-friendship with those you are teaching is an even bigger mistake still. As the great teacher blogger Andrew Old once wrote "The kids aren't there to solve your existential crisis. They are there to learn."[7]

Tip 5: Imagine yourself at the end of your career

A common tip which some life coaches give their clients is to imagine their own funeral. This can seem a little morbid but it is actually a very worthwhile exercise. What will be said when your eulogy is read? If someone were to write an obituary for you, what would go in it? This mode of thinking helps us to remember that we only get one shot at life so we had better make the very most of it.

Career wise, a parallel here would be to imagine your retirement party. If you've worked in schools for any length of time you have probably witnessed multiple times one of those emotional send offs for a school stalwart who has worked at that particular school for 20, 30 or even 40 years. The headteacher gives a short speech expressing their gratitude for this particular colleague's dedication, anecdotes are shared about the time that this teacher went through a whole assembly without realising that his jumper was on inside out and emotional colleagues holding paper plates of cocktail sausages and tuna sandwiches all gather round to say farewell.

Moments like this remind us just how potentially fulfilling and rewarding a career in teaching can be. Many teachers leaving the profession leave so many happy memories behind them. Throughout their time in the classroom, they will have touched the lives of literally thousands of young people. Many long-standing teachers even end up teaching the children of their ex-pupils. They become legends in their own communities and in some cases almost local celebrities. However, have a quick chat with one of these stalwarts and you will hear just how many teachers they have seen come and go over the years. Just because you pursue a teaching career over a number of decades, this does not guarantee you will achieve this very same happy ending and throughout the course of that 20, 30 or 40 year period, many other teachers will have decided quite rightly to move on and find an occupation more suited to them elsewhere. What's more, speak to any teacher veteran in your staff room and they will tell you that teaching is a significantly more difficult job today than it used to be and many will remark "I don't know how I'd cope if I was starting out today!"

Some people were born to be teachers and the job is just a perfect fit for them. If this is you then potentially you could find decades of happiness in teaching, although even then you need to make sure you find a school or college which fits. Very few people however do the exact same job for their whole life. If you choose to do this, you had better hope that that job fits you like a glove. I went in to teaching immediately after graduating from university and it was my first proper job. Because of this I had to ask myself: is this the only career that I ever want to try in life? Am I just so darned good at teaching that it would be a crime if I were to instead try and turn my hand to something else and see how that compares? The answer for me was no. People who hit on that perfect job first time around are a rare and lucky breed, as are those people who meet their soulmate at school and stay married to them until they are 95. Most of us aren't this lucky and need to do a bit of shopping around first before we find "the one".

Teaching has the potential to be a wonderful job and teachers are given a unique opportunity to affect and improve their local communities in a way that few other workers are. Having said that, no matter how hard you have worked, no matter how disadvantaged the pupils were whose lives you have improved, at the end of the day once those cocktail sausages and tuna sandwiches are cleared away you will be replaced and, eventually, forgotten. That's quite a big problem if you didn't even enjoy the ride in the first place.

Tip 6: Try to diagnose the cause of your current malaise
Since you're reading this book there's a fair chance that you feel somewhat dissatisfied in your current role. You'll most likely

find it incredibly useful then to spend a little time reflecting on why this might be.

One possibility is that you've found yourself in a setting that might not be that well suited to you. Every school and indeed every department is different and some settings just might not be right for you. There are hundreds of potential reasons why a particular school or department might not be a good fit. It would be impossible to list them all, but I hope that the list below will help you to think about some sources of potential conflict:

- Is discipline at this particular school especially poor? When you speak to colleagues who have worked at a number of different schools, how do they compare behaviour at your school to other schools they have worked in?
- Could you be working with pupils of the wrong age group?
- Is there a lack of camaraderie among you and your colleagues?
- Do you dislike the ethos of the school? Perhaps the management are only interested in examination results and nothing else?
- Are you facing the difficulty of working in a school which is in special measures?
- Do you sometimes feel like you might be teaching the wrong subject?
- Is there a culture of bullying among senior or middle management?
- Are you working in a school which has only opened recently and is still in the process of establishing itself?

It's hard to be sure sometimes exactly what the problem could be, so you may need to experiment. Perhaps try changing schools and then you will be changing several different variables at once. This will help you to get a better idea of whether there was something specific about your previous school which was causing you grief. The schools where the turnover of staff is the highest are often the schools which are the most likely to have cultural problems. If you come to the conclusion that the main source of your current dissatisfaction is the school, then you may well be in need of "option 2". There will be more advice on how to achieve this later.

Another possibility which you should consider is that possibility that there is something going on in your personal life which is impacting upon your professional life. As much as we may like to think so, our personal and professional lives rarely exist completely independently of one another. When we're experiencing success in our personal lives, this raises our morale and there is often a knock on effect in our work lives. Similarly, if things are tough at home and we arrive at work feeling frustrated, irritated or even miserable then this is likely to have an effect on how we perform at work. I think that this is especially true in teaching. Some jobs, like office jobs, are a little more forgiving when it comes to arriving at work in a bad mood. There's every chance that if you keep your head down then not too many people will notice. But with teaching you have to arrive a work ready to perform in front of a class every day. Children will be quick to detect that something is not right, and sometimes they can respond negatively to this.

Try to identify and correct any problems in your personal life which you think may be impacting upon your success at work. This way, you can see if it's in fact those problems which are the cause of your current malaise. I know that this is easier said than done! Sometimes you may feel that you are so snowed under with marking and planning that you don't have the time to work on some of the problems and issues you may have in your personal life. But this is a false economy. By taking your foot off the gas a little in your work related life and dedicating a little more time to your personal life, you may in fact increase your productivity and effectiveness in your job in the longer term.

Of course, it could be the case that any problems experienced in your personal life are in fact caused by the stress of your teaching job, and not the other way around. In cases like this, you can find yourself in a vicious circle if you're not careful. If you feel like your job is the cause of problems in your personal life, then taking a step out of the classroom even if only temporarily could be a good call. You will then have a little bit of breathing space to address the issues in your personal life and, who knows, once they are dealt with you could then make a return to teaching.

I think that one class of difficulties which deserves a special mention is mental health problems, especially depression and anxiety. These problems are all too common among teachers. If you're experiencing these issues then it could be that they are caused by the stress of teaching. It could also be that they are not caused by teaching but are having an impact on your effectiveness in the classroom or it could be a little bit of both. It doesn't matter what you may think (if anything) lies behind your mental health problems, if you think you are experiencing problems you owe it to yourself to go and have a conversation with your GP. Resolving these difficulties may be the key to resolving some of the difficulties you may be experiencing at work.

Another possibility is that it's not the school that's the problem nor is it issues in your personal life. It may be the case that, for one reason or another, you've just decided that teaching in *any* school isn't for you. This is the conclusion I came to myself and it can be a bitter pill to swallow.

As I said earlier, some people are born to be teachers. There is another category of people who absolutely are not meant to be teachers. These people realise pretty soon after entering the classroom that it isn't for them and hundreds of teachers either withdraw from or fail to pass their teacher training every year. But there is another category of teachers in the middle who I would call "moderately good teachers". I would probably place myself in this category. They're not necessarily the kinds of teachers whose inspiring influence is still felt a decade after one has been taught by them, but none the less they come in and they get the job done. Sometimes these moderately good teachers just end up burning out after years of the stress and demands of the teaching profession. Sometimes they get a little bit tired of teaching the same content year in and year out. And sometimes they get tired of being moderately good at their job and yearn to do something at which they feel they really excel.

There is no shame in being moderately good at something! All of us have things that we're very good at, things that we're moderately good at and things that we're absolutely atrocious at. Don't envy the teachers at your school who just seem to be able to do everything effortlessly. There will be plenty of other things in life that they're terrible at, I promise you! Whilst there is no shame at being only moderately good at something, there *is* I believe a certain degree of shame which ought to be legitimately felt by the person who persists in spending their life doing something which they are only moderately good at when the possibility exists for them to do something which they really excel at.

"But hang on a moment Mr Fletcher… you're missing something here. If you're moderately good at something then what you need to do is to work really hard at it and then you will improve. That way, something that you're moderately good at can become something which you genuinely excel at, right?"

In my honest opinion, this is largely wrong. I don't doubt for one moment that teachers can improve at their practice by learning from colleagues and experts. But I think that such improvements are likely to be marginal. This is especially true if one has already been teaching for more than a few years. All of us can learn to develop new talents and skills, but I believe that being a truly excellent teacher involves having a certain type of personality. Personalities can be shaped to some extent, but they can never be completely changed.

There is no better way to illustrate this than to look at the field of behaviour management. This is not a book about how to manage behaviour in a classroom, there are plenty of those already. But I have long observed that one's success in this particular area of practice is down in a large part to one's personality. Certain people just have a knack for it, and others just don't. Behaviour management books and courses sell the myth that anyone's behaviour management practice can be completely transformed. I don't doubt that it can be improved to some extent, but never transformed. Ask yourself this: have you ever known anyone who has been teaching for several years, who has a reputation for being not so great at behaviour management and then suddenly completely turns their situation around within a year or so? Conversely, have you ever known a teacher who has long been excellent at behaviour management who has suddenly lost their authority and started to experience poor discipline. I certainly haven't.

Any psychologist who is worth their salt will tell you that one of the surest paths to gratification and happiness in our lives is to find out what we truly excel at and make that an integral part of our daily lives. Few will advise that happiness consists in constantly confronting and struggling to correct our weaknesses. If you're a moderately good teacher and you don't have the opportunity to transition in to something which you truly excel at then be grateful that you are at least moderately good at what you currently do. But if the chance to do something which you do truly excel at is out there, is that a chance that you're willing to pass up?

I hope you are starting to get closer to making a decision about the future direction of your career. There is a seventh tip in my list, which is to get a clear overview of your current financial situation. Since money is such an important factor in any career change, I have decided to dedicate the next chapter of this book to it.

3. Money, Money, Money…

It's a shame to base any major decision in life on money, and I wouldn't advise that you do. But money is an important fact of life which we can't ignore.

If you're thinking about leaving teaching, my advice to you is to try and tighten your belt a little with immediate effect. By reducing your monthly spending you can achieve two things. First of all, you will be able to get some money saved in the bank. You may need some money in savings to rely on if you end up transitioning to a job which is not as well paid as your current one. But secondly, reducing your monthly spending a little should help you to realise that you are perfectly capable of living on a little less money that you are earning right now.

For me, leaving teaching has been one of the best decisions I have ever made. Since starting my new job I am much happier, less stressed and have much more time to spend with loved ones and on new hobbies and interests. But surely there must be some negatives, right?

Well, I think actually there have been very few negative aspects to my career change decision. But there is one cold hard fact which I can't deny. I earn considerably less money that I did before. I am not alone in this. According to a study of leaving teachers conducted by the National Foundation for Educational Research (NFER) in 2015[8], the wages of teachers who had left the profession were on average 10% lower than those who remained in the profession. The NFER claimed that there was "no sign of a significant minority of teachers leaving for better paid positons outside teaching in the state sector." A significant minority of teachers studied experienced a pay cut of more than 20%.

I think it is quite telling that so many teachers are leaving the profession and moving to lower paid jobs. To my mind, this illustrates that many teachers are rather unhappy in their jobs. But what are the potential financial implications of either continuing with teaching or treading a new path? Can you afford to leave? I hope to answer these questions in this chapter.

Is teaching a well-paid job?

Ask around in your staff round and you will hear a range of responses to this question. It is not an easy question to answer since not all teachers earn the same money.

According to recent Government figures, the average teacher's annual salary is £37,400.[9] One cannot dispute that this is considerably higher than the overall average income for all full time workers which was £27,200 in 2014.[10] Later on in this book I will recommend that those who are interested in a career change should go and discuss their options with a careers advisor. If you do, you may well find that they consider teaching to be a well-paid career on the whole.

Of course, many will disagree and it's not at all uncommon to hear teachers and teaching unions complain about teachers' salaries. There is no doubt that the insistence on only a 1% increase in pay each year for the past several years has been highly frustrating. What's more, as all teachers know, a salary of £37,400 or better is only achieved after several years in the profession. Statistics confirm that the *starting* salary in teaching is comparatively poor. The starting salary of £22,244 falls short of the average starting salary for all graduate jobs which was £27,000 in 2014 according to the Association of Graduate Recruiters.[11] Pay appears to be something which many people leaving teaching are unhappy with and in a recent survey of 591 teachers considering leaving the profession, 43% cited insufficient pay as a reason for wanting to leave.[12]

I've always felt that there is something a little odd about the pay scale in teaching since in my experience the job becomes slightly easier, if anything, the longer one has been doing it. We all remember just how tough our NQT year was. This may well have been the year of our teaching career during which we put in the most effort yet we got the lowest salary for it. As time goes by and we build up a bank of ideas, resources and experiences the whole process of planning and delivering lessons becomes a little easier. In some ways, the amount of effort we have to put in is inversely proportional to how much we earn. As I mentioned in the introduction, the pay system can seem at times as if it has been designed to trap you. The longer you've been a teacher, the less likely it can seem you would be able to find a similar salary elsewhere. But you're only ever trapped if you perceive yourself to be, and that decision is entirely yours.

Just as teachers look like they're starting to get comfortable with the demands of their jobs, they often then boost their earnings by taking on extra responsibilities in order to earn themselves a TLR payment. I must admit, during my own teaching career I often questioned how wise this really was. Responsibilities such as head of year or head of department will earn you a little more money, but these responsibilities often involve a *lot* more work. I always urge any teacher who is planning a step up to think very carefully about whether they really need the extra money and whether the extra stress and workload will really be worth it in the end. All too many teachers let their ambition run away with them and some of them live to regret it in the end.

I believe that when you're starting out as a NQT you're in a situation which is poor value for money when you consider how much you are earning in comparison to how much effort you're putting in. I think the same can be true of those who find themselves in positions of responsibility. The pay is high, but the demands of the job are even higher. Could it be that there is a perfect sweet spot somewhere in the middle? If one focusses on just teaching and doesn't take on responsibilities then one can still earn £37,871[1] at the top of the upper pay scale. To me, this always felt like the best "value" option when balancing pay against workload.

There are of course two ways of looking at pay – you can look at total annual salary or you can look at money earnt for every hour of work. When we're comparing one sector against another, we often only look at the total annual figure. However, if we start to think in terms of amount of money earnt per hour, then it may become an awful lot easier to leave the teaching profession without taking a pay cut. Let's imagine the "average" teacher. They earn £37,400. The NFER report[8] I mentioned earlier concluded that on average those teachers leaving the profession were taking a pay cut of 10%. This takes our salary down to £33,660. Now if we look at teachers' working hours and consider everything, that is we consider that teachers get a lot of holiday but consider also that teachers spend some time working during these holidays, teachers work on average 48.3 hours per week across the whole year.[13] This compares to the average for all full-time occupations which is 39.1 hours.[14]

A quick calculation with these figures confirms that a teacher on an average salary who works the average number of hours that a teacher works earns £14.89 per hour for their efforts. If they were to leave and take a 10% pay cut but work "normal" full time hours, their hourly rate would in fact increase to £16.55! So what at first appears to be a 10% pay cut actually ends up being an 11% pay rise! In fact, a teacher could drop to a salary as low as £30,274 (a 19% drop) and still earn the same hourly rate so long as they were only working 39.1 hours per week as opposed to 48.3 hours per week. Certainly some food for thought!

One should also consider not just one's starting salary in their new job but also where it could go in future. Any career change from any sector will often involve a pay cut as one moves from the top or the middle of one pay scale to the bottom of another. But after a few years in a new profession, progression and promotion often mean that one can match or even exceed their previous salary. When factoring money in to your career decision, you must again refer to some of the personal values you identified earlier. You will need to think about how important money is to you in the grand scheme of things. Is it more or less important than free time, time for hobbies and time to spend with your children? For me, money is quite low down on my list of priorities. However, there is absolutely no shame in being someone who makes it a higher priority.

Give yourself a financial audit

I suggested earlier that it is a good idea to start to reduce your spending. What I think is also a good idea is to complete a quick financial audit just so that you can get a grip of your monthly spending. This will help you to see how much money you *need* which is often a different figure to how much money you'd *like* to have in your account each month ideally.

When it comes to money, there is an extent to which we each cut our own cloth according to our own needs. In other words, we each adjust to how much money we have and we learn to live on that amount of money. Sometimes when we get a pay rise we don't feel any richer as we adjust our lifestyles accordingly and so we still don't seem to ever have any money left at the end of the month. But if we can quickly adjust upwards then we can just as quickly adjust downwards, however there has to be enough money available for the essentials!

Evaluating your household budget isn't rocket science. I recommend creating a simple Excel spreadsheet listing all of your essential monthly outgoings. Find a cell where you can enter your monthly income and then a simple subtraction will give you a feel for what disposable wealth you have each month. It goes without saying that you should pay off any debts that you have ASAP. If debt is making your financial life difficult, you may consider putting your career change on the back burner whilst you sort out that issue first. Once your finances are straight you will be in a better position to think about the possibility of affording a pay cut. Below is the simple spreadsheet I created. Feel free to email me if you would like me to send you a template as an attachment.

	A	B
1	Monthly takehome:	1950
2		
3	Mortgage	647
4	Council tax	71.16
5	Gas and Electric	37
6	Water	21.97
7	Mobile Phone	15.19
8	TV licence	12.13
9	Broadband	28.25
10	Food	152.14
11	Gym	18.99
12		
13	Total monthly out	1003.83
14	Monthly disposable	946.17
15		

Money saving and making tips

A career change could involve a reduction in your monthly income, but there could be some adjustments you could make which could in fact make your career change work in your favour financially.

Firstly, there could be some costs associated with teaching which you no longer have to pay anymore. A good example are union subscription fees. Stopping paying these could save you over £200 per year. If you leave teaching mid-way through a subscription year, don't forget to cancel your subscription payments. Of course, you may choose to join a union in your new career but you may find that you move to a job where the crucial legal protection which union membership gives you isn't actually required.

Secondly, you should take a career change as on opportunity to re-evaluate your pension arrangements. Almost all teachers opt in to the Teachers' Pension Scheme. It is renowned for being a generous pension plan. Whilst your employer will be paying a lot in to your pension, if you check your latest payslip you may be surprised at just how much you are paying in to it yourself. Once you're getting towards the higher end of the pay scale, your contributions could be well over 10%. If you're taking a pay cut, you may wish to cushion the blow by reducing or even eliminating pension contribution even if only temporarily. Depending on your age and circumstances, there might not be anything wrong with taking a 2 or 3 year break from paying in to a pension to help you through a difficult time. Just make sure that 2 or 3 years doesn't turn in to 20 or 30 years!

Something else you should consider is how much you are spending each year on commuting. Many teachers are smart enough not to live in the catchment areas they serve. If this is you and you can find new work closer to home this could save you a fortune at the petrol pump. If you can find a position where you would be able to cycle to work, all the better.

As well as finding ways to save money, you could also think about ways that you could supplement a lower wage in a new career through self-employment. As I mentioned earlier, teachers work significantly more hours than most other workers. If your career change leaves you with more free time, perhaps you could take on some private tutoring to earn some extra cash? Taking on pupils for tutoring would mean that you could continue to use those skills you have developed in your school career. It would help you stay "in touch" with any developments in the curriculum which would be very useful should you ever chose to return to the classroom. For many teachers, tutoring is great fun and it allows them to share their love of learning but without the headache of behaviour management, paperwork and Ofsted. Thanks to the internet it is easier to advertise and get started than ever before. Sites such as Gumtree and Tutor Hunt will allow you to list adverts for free and if you're good, news of this can spread very quickly through word of mouth. There are tutoring agencies you can sign up for who can find you work. These will take a cut, but this is a good way to get started and build a client base. There may be some centres in your local area which offer after school services to local school pupils who may consider taking you on too. Another possibility nowadays is even online tutoring, often done from the comfort of one's home using a webcam. This is very much an emerging technology and you may find it harder to get pupils compared to the more traditional route, however your potential client base isn't just limited to those in your local community – you could tutor pupils on the other side of the world!

Nowadays, there also exists the opportunity for you to make money from publishing education related resources you have made. The Times Educational Supplement website allows authors to upload their resources and sell them for cash. This could give you the perfect opportunity to monetise all of that hard work you have put in over the years making materials for use in the classroom. Continuing on the publishing theme, some textbook and revision book publishers such as CGP also actively seek submissions from teachers for their publications. Keep your eye on publishers' websites for news of opportunities.

If you're prepared to put in a bit of time during evening and weekends, you could also consider working part time as an examiner or moderator for one of the main examination boards. There are usually plenty of vacancies in this field and often exam scripts can be marked from the comfort of your sofa, so long as you have a laptop to hand!

I hope you're now starting to get a good idea of whether you'd like to remain in teaching, whether you feel you need to make a few adjustments or whether you'd like to try something else entirely. The next chapter will look at some of the adjustments which a teacher could make to potentially reduce their stress levels whilst remaining in the teaching profession.

4. Making Adjustments

If you're not quite sure whether a full blown career change is for you and you feel like you're not quite ready to leave the classroom, then you may be considering what I referred to earlier as "option 2". This was to stay in teaching but at the same time try and make some sort of significant change to your predicament to increase your level of job satisfaction. This could be a useful way to diagnose and rule out certain causes of your current dissatisfaction.

It may be the case that a change is just what you need and after your adjustment you may experience a new lease of life and years of job satisfaction. Considering some kind of change could be especially important if you've been working in the same environment for a long time or if you've only ever worked in one school or college. Making an adjustment could also be a useful gateway to what I call "option 3" – leaving the profession entirely. Sometimes you need to make a change and try something else within teaching just to convince yourself once and for all that teaching really isn't for you. Then you can leave safe in the knowledge that you're making the right decision. There are many different adjustments to be made and I will list as many as I possibly can in this chapter.

Working part time

A discussion of part time work follows on nicely from a discussion about money, so I've decided to cover this one first. In a recent survey of teachers who were considering leaving the profession, 76% of those teachers cited high workload as a reason for wanting to leave.[12] It's no wonder that with such a crippling workload, countless teachers yearn to work part time. If you're main aim is to shift your work life balance firmly back in the "life" direction, going part time is surely an effective way to achieve this.

Obviously one of the main considerations when considering going part time is whether one can afford to. Part time work is usually a viable option when there is another full time (or perhaps even part time) wage earner in the household. For teachers with children, part time work is a great way to allow at least one parent (and it doesn't necessarily have to be Mummy!) to spend a little bit more time with their offspring and takes away some of the stress of juggling child-rearing with full time work. The dilemma of extra money vs. extra time is a tough one, and if you have children you may assume that what they really want most is a bumper sack of presents at Christmas and exotic foreign holidays every year. However you shouldn't underestimate how much they will value spending time with you, especially if they are still young.

I should mention also some more unconventional approaches to part time work. Sometimes it might be assumed that part time work is only for those in a couple, only for those with children or even only for women. But yet there is no rule book that stipulates any of these things. If you're on the average teacher salary of £37,400, couldn't you in fact survive on 80% of that salary as opposed to 100% of that salary, even if you are on your own?

Such a move would still place you on a salary which is above average in the grand scheme of things. Since the average teacher is now working over 50 hours per week during term time, cutting down to a 0.8 timetable might just end up allowing you to work the kind of normal full time hours that people typically work in many other industries. You might worry that such a move will make you look odd, eccentric or lazy. People might ask you *why* you work part time, as if there has to be some sort of special justification for such a lifestyle. But remember that rational decisions about your career should be based on what helps to best meet your own personal happiness and well-being, not what best pleases others. If you do choose to go part time and other people judge you, let them judge. In the longer term they won't be judging you, they will be envying you.

If you think you might want to go part time, begin with a simple conversation with your headteacher. They may say no, but you will have lost nothing. If there aren't any part time opportunities available at that particular moment, they can at least keep your request in the back of their minds for the future. If it's becoming clear you're going to have to move on then set up a jobs alert on the TES website. Do remember of course that all schools are not equal. You can't guarantee that a part time timetable in a tricky school environment will be any easier than a full time timetable in a better environment. Since you *can* be sure that the part time school will pay you less, you should always make any decision carefully.

Changing sector

One way to give your career a bit of a shakeup is to change sectors. I'm thinking here predominantly about a move from the state sector to the independent sector.

There are many differences between these two sectors and there are pros and cons of both. For teachers who have spent the entirety of their careers so far in the state sector, it might be worth sampling some of the pros of the independent sector first before deciding to throw in the towel entirely. Every independent school is different and I could be accused of making some generalisations here but on the whole, many teachers find that discipline is less of an issue in the independent sector and that there are fewer pupils who have a poor attitude to learning. Since they are investing in their children's education financially, parents of pupils in independent schools typically put of lot of pressure on their children to do well and succeed. Just as they have high expectations of their children, independent school parents will also have very high expectations of the teachers whose salaries their fees are paying so you should be prepared for that too. Class sizes in the independent sector are sometimes smaller and timetables usually contain a few more free periods. Both of these things have the effect of reducing marking workloads.

There can be some extra perks of working in independent schools such as free cooked meals, although don't assume that pay is necessarily any higher than it is in the state sector. Whilst holidays in the independent sector are typically longer, so too is the school day and teachers are often expected to stay behind after school regularly to take part in clubs and extra-curricular activities. Independent schools don't just want to take on teachers who might be struggling in their state school and you need to have something to bring to the table, especially in terms of contributing to the school's extra-curricular programme. Having said that, transferring from the state to the independent sector is not uncommon and often the lesson planning abilities of state school teachers are highly admired by independent schools.

When asked why they have never worked or considered working in independent schools, many state school teachers will cite philosophical reasons and say that they disagree with the very notion of privately funded education. I totally understand this and we should be very grateful that all teachers aren't only interested in working in the independent sector or else where would we be? However, as someone who has always worked in an inner-city state school, people who I talk to from the independent sector can sometimes be surprised by my ethical views. They often tell me that they can feel a little guilty about what they do and that they admire me for taking a more ethical route in my career. However I point out to them that actually I do not consider everything that is done in state schools to be particularly ethical. In my experience, the current trend in state schools is that they appear to be interested in examination performance, league tables and Ofsted judgments to the exclusion of just about everything else. Pupils' mental well-being and their moral and personal development usually seem to take the back seat and something I admire about many fee paying schools is the way they seem to take a more rounded approach to that currently taken in state schools. Whatever your views on the ethics of the two different sectors, remember that the answers to ethical questions of any kind are rarely black and white.

What's more, if you're ruling out a move to the independent sector for ethical reasons, remember that this could be a strange decision if you then end up leaving teaching all together and end up working a different job in the private sector. All educators are doing something ethical ultimately.

Changing school

Less radical than changing sectors is changing schools. This could be an incredibly simple way to kick start your career. No two schools are the same. There are so many different factors which can vary from one school to the next: culture and ethos, the standard of behaviour, marking policies, facilities, quality of management and so on. A school change, executed correctly, can save a flagging career. On the other hand, get a school change wrong and it could prove to be the final nail in the coffin.

I worked for many years at a school with a high turnover and have seen many a school move go wrong. Why did they go wrong? Almost always because the teachers who were moving did not spend enough time researching their new schools. Sometimes teachers make school moves in haste. This can be because they are in a desperately unhappy situation and just can't wait to leave their existing school. Other times teachers get itchy feet and are desperate to get a promotion. They go to the first school which offers any kind of promotion and later question whether that extra £150 per month in their pay packet was really worth it.

If you're changing schools, don't rush and do your homework. Of course you will do the obvious things like look at the results and will perhaps read the most recent Ofsted report. But you must do more than this. You can never truly know what life will be like day in and day out at a particular school until you have worked there, but the next best thing you can do is to *speak to someone who either works there currently or has worked there recently*. There is no substitute for this. If you've been teaching even only a few years then chances are you'll have a network of teacher friends and hopefully you can find either a friend or a friend of a friend who has experience of the particular school you're interested in, even if that experience is only being placed there during a PGCE year. All schools have a reputation in their communities one way or another but when thinking about reputations remember that just because a school has a reputation for being a good place for parents to send their children to this does not mean that it is necessarily a fantastic place to work as a teacher. Sometimes the very opposite is true!

Visit any school before you apply. It may be the case that during this visit there is an extent to which the school is sizing you up and deciding whether they would like to employ you. At the same time, you should be thinking about whether *you* are prepared to consider offering this place the fantastic set of skills which you have. Don't be fooled by appearances. Just because a school is operating from a brand new multi-million pound building and just because the headteacher has recently introduced a smart new blazer as part of the uniform these are not things which you ought to be taking all that seriously. The atmosphere inside classrooms and corridors and the morale of the staff are far more important things to consider.

One last point I'd like to make is that you don't have to be getting promoted in order to move schools. If you fancy a move, then move. I've often been told that so called "sideways moves" might often be treated with some kind of suspicion. If your new potential employer wants to look at your move with suspicion, let them! The worst that can happen is that you don't get appointed, at which point you can dust yourself off and begin work on your next application.

Supply teaching

A common piece of advice I hear given to those teachers who are considering a career change is "why don't you do a bit of supply for a while, this could help to ease you through the transition." I don't always fully understand this advice.

In my own case, I had been working in my teaching job for many years. I began to become unhappy and decided I was going to leave. I researched new jobs thoroughly and found one I wanted to apply for. I discussed my intentions with my headteacher and then applied and luckily I was successful. I then sat down with my headteacher and we discussed notice periods and came to an agreement. Job done. Staying in my existing job the whole time had two clear advantages – I maintained a steady stream of reliable income and when I was approaching potential new employers my CV showed that I was currently in a steady job which I had been doing for many years rather than something casual and temporary. It felt like I was leaving from a position of strength.

Supply teaching isn't easy. Pupils don't always tend to respect supply teachers as much as regular teachers and you could find yourself fighting tough battles day in and day out if you're not careful. The quality and suitability of work set by absent teachers can vary enormously. Whilst the pay you can get for a day's work is reasonable, you are not guaranteed regular work and what's more you won't get paid during the school holidays. There are some clear advantages though – mainly the lack of marking and planning. When that bell rings at 3.30p.m, that's it. Supply teachers who are successful and get a good reputation are often invited by schools to fill in for a particular absent teacher over a longer period, perhaps a half term or two. This will leave you with more stability, but then with that stability comes the dreaded marking and planning and before you know it you're back where you started. Secondary supply work can sadly often just be about crowd control. With primary, you can expect less crowd control but more hands on interaction helping pupils.

However, primary supply teachers may be expected to get their hands dirty and do some marking even if they are only in a particular school for one day.

One advantage of moving to supply teaching is that you then can leave without serving a long notice period. Having said that, remember that your current headteacher may be more flexible with respect to leaving dates than your contract suggests and in my case I decided to just cross that bridge when I came to it. One situation in which I might suggest supply teaching as an option is when you have decided that you are going to leave teaching and are so utterly miserable in your current job that it is becoming a struggle to drag yourself in to work each day whilst still clinging on to some semblance of sanity. If things are getting really tough, supply work could offer you something of a breather.

If you want to do supply, your best bet is most likely to sign up with an agency in your local area, many of whom will be quite keen to snap up qualified teachers. If you're doing supply whilst looking for a new career, you might even deliberately keep one day each week clear so that you can dedicate that day to job hunting and writing applications. Is it possible for supply teaching to become a viable long term career option? Never say never, but it would seem that the consensus here is that supply teaching is quite a tough gig to sustain in the longer term. Remember that an alternative to supply teaching is to work as a cover supervisor. Cover supervisors are often employed permanently by one school. There is more stability in terms of pay but it will almost certainly be less in per hour terms. Being in the same school all the time may mean you are taken a little more seriously by pupils and you will have the chance to establish a reputation for yourself around the school. A job like this may be a better long term proposition than traditional supply teaching.

Taking a demotion

I saw many young teachers arrive at my old school over the years. I witnessed a certain pattern emerging. They would work for two, maybe three years and then would decide that they must now seek a promotion. I don't believe that the motivation was primarily money, rather it was a sense of egotism and a desire to succeed and achieve. Seeking promotion was the done thing. One copied one's peers – they had achieved a promotion, so why shouldn't I?

I must admit I never found the idea of promotion all that alluring. Why? Because I thought that teaching my classes was already a full time job. For each of my classes I wanted to be able to prepare their lessons thoroughly and mark their work and once I had done this (oh, and also teach them too) there just didn't seem to be any time left. I didn't understand how those with responsibilities coped and it often seemed to some extent that they only did cope by cutting certain corners with some aspects of their main teaching job.

We can all agree that teaching is a tough job with a high workload. Why do so many teachers insist on making their jobs even tougher by taking on more and more? When I was a school pupil myself, it seemed that all of the heads of year at my school tended to be old, experienced teachers. It amazes me nowadays how young many people with positions of responsibility are, in fact I've even known NQTs to take on such positions. Such is the culture in schools nowadays, careers are short since teachers burn out after a few years and there are few oldies left to take on these important tasks.

If you've taken on a position of responsibility and lived to regret it, there is no shame in taking a step back down the ladder if that's what you genuinely want to do. Priorities in life change. Perhaps when you started climbing the ladder you did so because you harboured ambitions to get to the top (or near to the top) of it. But if this ambition has now changed, wouldn't it be easier to step on to a lower rung? Some teachers seem to think that such a move is impossible, or they worry what their colleagues will think of them. A message which I keep trying to hammer home in this book is that rational decisions about your career are ones which are based on your own interests and happiness, not on a desire to impress others. Even if you do take a step down, such a decision is not irreversible and you can always change your mind again at some point in the future.

Money wise, I'll repeat again my belief that the teachers who are perhaps getting the best value when one compares salary against workload are those teachers who are at the top of the pay scale but yet have no responsibilities. You do get a little more for taking on extra work, but is it worth it and do you really need it? A good way to keep perspective too is to remind yourself how long you might have left in teaching. Let's say you're 40. You might not retire until you're 65. You could take a five year break from responsibility and were you then to step back up again after that five year break you could still stay up there for another 20 years!

Changing phase

Of all of the possibilities in this section, this is perhaps one of the hardest to implement. By changing phase, I mean changing the age of the pupils you typically work with. The easiest of all phase changes to make would probably be to change from a traditional secondary setting to a further education setting which focuses only on 16-19 pupils. This could certainly be doable, especially if you've got a lot of experience teaching sixth form under your belt. Even if you haven't, it could be worth making a few enquiries.

Changing from primary to secondary or vice versa could be a little trickier, although it is not impossible. Officially, "Qualified Teacher Status" applies equally across all phases so whichever phase you're currently working in you are at least qualified on paper to work in another. Of the two transitions, primary to secondary would be easier than secondary to primary. This is because the jobs market in primary is generally tougher.

There could be some good news for you if you do dream of moving from primary to secondary. A bulge in the birth rate a few years ago has led to a bulge in numbers entering primary just recently. Unsurprisingly, this is going to lead to a bulge in numbers hitting secondary schools a few years down the line. There are some quite serious concerns about whether secondary schools will be ready for this. More teachers are needed in secondary, yet in 2015 the number of teachers who left the profession in fact exceeded the number who joined.[5] In the NFER's recent report in to this problem,[8] one of the recommendations made was that Government should consider allowing a "greater flexibility between phases". It is therefore possible that some primary teachers could be encouraged in to secondary simply because of the sheer scale of this numbers problem.

The prospects of a teacher trying to move from secondary to primary could be slim as such a teacher could face stiff competition from those with more relevant experience. A good first step might be to try and do some primary supply work. Those with certain subject specialisms which are sought after in primary, such as maths, could have an advantage. Teachers trying to make a move like this should build up as many contacts as possible. Sometimes when you're trying to make a more unconventional career move, you need someone who you can call on to do you a favour.

Teaching abroad

Packing up one's suitcases and moving abroad to teach seems to be an increasingly popular option for teachers nowadays, so much so that recently Ofsted chief Sir Michael Wilshaw decided to dedicate one of his trademark whinges to this very subject.[15]

Europe, Asia and the Middle East are all popular destinations for adventurous British teachers who have become disillusioned with the culture of British schools and the associated lifestyle. It's not difficult to find schools abroad which teach the English school curriculum and you won't necessarily have to learn a new language. Many of these schools are private schools and working there comes with all the perks of the independent sector mentioned earlier. There are many agencies who actively try to recruit British teachers on behalf of schools abroad who can help you with your job search. A recent BBC news article gives an interesting account of a number of different teachers who have decide to take the plunge.[16] Most teachers who have made such a move will say typically that when one considers the whole package of pay, conditions and workload the situation is a lot more favourable in international schools than it is in British schools. I know of not one teacher who has taught in an international school and has reported that the conditions there are less favourable overall. Since salaries can be high and accommodation costs are sometimes taken care of, moving abroad can provide an excellent opportunity to save money and some teachers may find on their return to the UK they can at last get themselves on the housing ladder, something which was once a distant dream. Being on the housing ladder already however needn't stop you from going and there is no reason why you can't get an agent to let out your property while you're away.

For those teachers in couples, moving away can be a joint adventure and for singletons it can be an opportunity to find love in a new place. Those who choose to travel often have a "carpe diem" type attitude, although it is worth taking a little time to think about possible plans for once your overseas teaching journey is over (unless of course it never ends!).

5. Researching and Finding a New Career

If options 1 and 2 are off the table, that takes us to option 3 – getting out of teaching entirely. We will now look at some of the steps required to make an "escape".

The very worst thing you can do is to rush the process of researching a new career. If you're unhappy with your current job this can be tempting. Sometimes when you're having a bad day at work it will seem like *anything* would be better. But the last thing you want to do is to step out of the frying pan and in to the fire. As I mentioned earlier, if you *are* unhappy in your current job then one possibility (although this isn't always true) is that you didn't research your existing career quite well enough. As Einstein pointed out, doing the same thing twice and expecting different results is the very definition of insanity. You need to research your new career as thoroughly as possible because if you keep doing what you've always done, you'll keep getting what you've always gotten.

Changing careers is a big moment in your life and as with all big moments like moving house, planning a wedding or deciding to have children, you have to accept that it's a big decision which will take time and a lot of careful consideration. But what is the process you should go through to make sure you find the right career for you?

What jobs do ex-teachers do?

I've talked a few times in this book about a report which was published recently (2015) by the National Foundation for Educational Research (NFER) which studied those who have left the teaching profession.[8] This is actually quite a short report and one which I would suggest you might find useful to read. One of the most interesting things in this report is that it offers a breakdown of the destinations of those who have left the teaching profession. Using the Government's Labour Force Survey, the NFER looked at a sample of 936 teachers who had left teaching between 2001 and 2015. The sample does not include teachers who have chosen to retire. The pie chart below summarises the destinations of those leaving teaching.

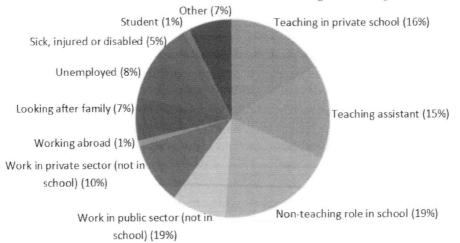

Other (7%)
Student (1%)
Sick, injured or disabled (5%)
Unemployed (8%)
Looking after family (7%)
Working abroad (1%)
Work in private sector (not in school) (10%)
Work in public sector (not in school) (19%)
Teaching in private school (16%)
Teaching assistant (15%)
Non-teaching role in school (19%)

The most encouraging thing about this data is that only 8% of leaving teachers turn out to be unemployed. One of the most interesting things about the data is that is shows that the majority of teachers who leave still end up remaining in the education sector in some form. Only 10% of teachers take up non-school jobs in the private sector. This indicates that transitioning to a different sector entirely could be tricky, but it is certainly possible.

Perhaps one of the first things you should consider then is whether you would like to remain in the education sphere or not. I will consider education related careers in detail in the next chapter, but for now I will continue to discuss more generally how to research possible careers.

Get some careers advice

If you're planning on changing career, you'd be silly not to spend a little time talking through your options with a trained professional. I can guarantee that you will have access to at least one free source of careers advice, and most likely two.

Your first port of call for advice should be the Government sponsored National Careers Service. You can find their website at http://nationalcareersservice.direct.gov.uk. I found this website to be extremely useful. Especially useful for me were the collection of job profiles. There are hundreds of jobs and careers described on the website and in each case you can find out exactly what the job entails as well as learn about possible routes in to that particular line of work and a list of the qualifications that you will require. Searching through the job profiles is a good first step but once you've done this I recommend that you arrange to actually speak to a careers advisor to get advice tailored to your circumstances. You can speak to an advisor online, on the phone or you can make an appointment to speak to someone in person. The advisor can also help you to put together your own careers action plan and email it to you. You'll also find on the website a tool to help you develop your CV. This can be very useful since it could be a while since you've had to write one!

You know that chunk of money which gets taken from your pay slip every month to repay your student loan? Annoying isn't it? Well now it's time to start taking advantage of the fact that you're an alumnus of your university and make full use of their services! All universities operate careers advice services. These are intended primarily for current students of the university but if you check your university's website you will most likely find that as an alumnus you are also entitled to use the university careers service for free! If you did your undergraduate degree and your PGCE at two different places then you may even have two different universities to choose from. These university careers services will typically make available free careers advice appointments which you can book. The advice will be geared towards people such as yourself who hold degree qualifications.

Another option is to pay for a careers advisor to help you. You may even be able to find one who specialises in career changes as opposed to one who tends to help out those starting out in the workplace. Your university careers service may be able to point you in the direction of one of these. Professional careers advice could be expensive, but do remember that you spend the majority of your waking life at work! You most likely will have tens of thousands of hours in the workplace left ahead of you so bear that in mind when you're deliberating over either paying for some careers advice or investing in a new iPad.

Make a shortlist of possibilities

Something I found useful was to open up a simple Microsoft Word document and make a list of all of the jobs I might consider doing. It's important to be as open-minded as possible here. Any job that might pop in to your head is worth noting down no matter how odd it might seem or how unlikely it might seem that you could end up doing it. Save this document and then any time a new idea pops in to your head you can note it down. This document can serve two purposes – it has a practical purpose in that it helps you to think about the sorts of jobs that you might like to apply for but you can also use this list to pick you up a little if you're ever feeling deflated. Sometimes during your job search you may become prone to pessimism and start to think that you will never find anything, but your list should remind you that there are in fact many jobs out there which you could potentially do. You just need a little patience and you'll get there in the end.

Network

Often the best way to find a new career opportunity is to put your face about and actually get out there and speak to people.

I hope that you have many friends and relatives who aren't teachers. What do they do? When you're in the process of looking for a new job take every opportunity you get to speak to others about their careers. Ask them what they do, ask them how they got in to it, ask them whether they would recommend it and ask them if they could give you a hand in getting in to their line of work. The worst that can happen is that they say no.

Many jobs aren't advertised but instead just get given to relatives, friends, or friends of friends. This is especially true of small companies who often don't want the expense of advertising. Some of your friends may do jobs that you didn't even know existed and which don't necessarily appear on a careers advisor's list of possible careers. If you're doing some research of your own about a possible new career, do try and speak to someone in that industry before you apply for and accept a job in that industry. If you don't know anyone, you could even see if there are any relevant online forums where you can speak to people who are doing the job you're interested in now. Being offered a new job is always exciting and flattering but always make sure you know what you are letting yourself in for. If someone were to ask me whether I would recommend a career in teaching, to be perfectly frank I would probably say no. Yet there are no doubt hundreds of young teachers who will be going in to the profession every year without ever asking anyone that question.

Search for jobs online

The days of having to wait for the particular day's newspaper which has the jobs section in are long gone. The internet is by far the best place to find job adverts nowadays, although don't rule out starting on the website of your local newspaper!

There are two main ways to search for jobs online. The first way is to search on one of the big job search sites. These are sites such as indeed.co.uk and monster.co.uk which aggregate jobs from many different employers all in one place. Some of these sites even enable you to upload your CV to them giving employers the potential to find you (although I wouldn't hold your breath on this one!). The second way to find jobs is to go direct to the site of a particular employer that you are interested in. You need to realise that not all jobs are advertised on the big sites. A company or organisation can upload an advert to their own website at no cost whatsoever and so this is a good first place to advertise.

The big job sites are useful for browsing and you will find them useful if you are yet to narrow your focus. However once you have narrowed your focus a little and have more of a specific idea about the kind of job you want, you then may find it more fruitful to head direct to the places which interest you. Once you've got a list of sites that you're keeping your eye on, try to check these sites for new jobs at least once a week.

Some organisation's websites may have a search facility on their jobs page, even though they may only have a few hundred jobs on there at most. The problem sometimes with job searching on websites is that you have to know exactly what job title you're searching for. Sometimes you may only have a rough idea of the sort of job you want, and often two different organisations will list the same role under different job titles. A good way around this is to leave the search box empty and press search, this way you can browse all the jobs. It's possible that you may have to press the spacebar first if the site doesn't allow a completely empty search box.

When it comes to scrutinising job adverts, you need to pay most attention to which skills the employer is looking for and what experience they are after. There will be more later on the specific skills you have developed as a teacher. You may find that you can rule out over 90% of all the jobs you look at straight away, however you mustn't get discouraged. Job hunting is a numbers game and you may have to sift through hundreds of adverts before you find the right job. Remember that in the end, for a job search to be successful you only need to get *one* employer to accept you.

Don't forget the power of being pro-active too. Even if there aren't any jobs advertised at an organisation which interests you it only takes two minutes to send them an email. Why not get a template email saved at the ready in your drafts folder with your carefully crafted CV attached?

Here is a list of some of the big job search sites which you may find useful to help you get started:

www.indeed.co.uk

www.monster.co.uk

www.reed.co.uk

www.fish4jobs.co.uk

www.jobsite.co.uk

www.totaljobs.com

www.cv-library.co.uk

Don't rule out graduate schemes

If you're a teacher then you're most likely a graduate too. One good way to help you think about what career you would like next is to turn back the clock in your mind and imagine you're 21 again and graduating from university. Suppose that teaching as a career option is off the table. What would you have chosen to do?

Many graduates who don't go in to teaching often end up doing graduate schemes. When I first started contemplating a career change, finding one of these schemes to enrol in was one of the first possibilities I considered. However, I was soon disappointed. I found that in most cases, when companies or organisations say "graduate" what they really mean is "recent graduate". Different organisations seem to have different ideas about what constitutes "recent" but you'll be lucky if you can find a scheme which will accept you if you graduated more than five years ago. This did annoy me a little – why was I being punished for having more life experience than other candidates?

Some readers, for example disgruntled NQTs may find that they are still in fact recent graduates. If this is you, graduate schemes could be well worth your consideration and often rates of pay are rather competitive. Many employers are a little picky at what degree you have and if you don't have at least a 2.1 this may well rule you out of most schemes. Whilst many organisations are after recent graduates, this is not true of *all* schemes and if you search hard you may be able to find some employers who value the skills you have developed since you left university. One notable example I have found is the NHS management graduate scheme which seems to be fairly flexible in its entry requirements.

6. Non-Teaching Jobs in Education

The research I cited in the previous chapter indicated that approximately half of all teachers who leave teaching jobs in state schools remain working in the education sector. If you're leaving teaching, a job which is still within the education sector is well worth your consideration.

There are several advantages to staying in the broader education sphere. Firstly, you're sticking with what you know. There's a good chance that in your new job you will still be using not just the skills which you developed during your time as a teacher but also the knowledge too. Secondly, you most likely have a network of contacts within the education world and these may be able to help you get your foot in the door in another role. Finally, by remaining in the education sector you make it a little bit easier to return to your old role as a teacher should you ever decide to. Whilst thousands of teachers leave the profession every year, there are also thousands who choose to return as well.

In this chapter I will profile some of the non-teaching jobs available in the education world. This list is by no means exhaustive, but I hope that it may give you a few useful ideas.

Teaching assistant jobs

More ex-teachers take on jobs as teaching assistants than any other role. This isn't that surprising – there are clearly many similarities between the two roles. In fact, research also shows that many people who train to be teachers used to be teaching assistants, so there is a flow of people in both directions.

By working as a teaching assistant you can enjoy many of the advantages of being a teacher but without many of the hassles. You still get the enjoyment of working with children and helping them to succeed. What you lose is the marking, planning and admin. Your working hours would be dramatically reduced and you could enjoy putting your feet up every evening and weekend. As a former teacher, you would most likely be an especially effective teaching assistant as you have a unique understanding of what assistance teachers need most in their lessons. What's more, when it comes to applying for jobs there's every chance that your application will make it to the top of the pile.

Well, this all sounds too good to be true, doesn't it? As you've probably already realised, being a teaching assistant is a very poorly paid job. Teaching assistants often don't get paid full time salaries, and they almost always don't get paid for school holidays. Remember, school holidays alone account for one quarter of the entire year. Salaries for teaching assistants in adverts are already low, and since you are then only paid "pro-rata" the salary becomes even lower still. Whilst some higher level teaching assistants can earn a little more, it is highly unlikely that any teaching assistant would be able to support themselves financially if theirs was the only salary coming in to their household.

Being a teaching assistant can be a lovely job but it all depends on your personal circumstances as to whether you can afford to do it. If there is another income coming in to your household or if you happen to have a lot of money in the bank, then life as a TA could be your ticket to a lower stress life. If you have some money in the bank which you could use to supplement a TA income for a few years, then perhaps you could work as a teaching assistant for a while to give yourself a short break from the teaching profession before making a return again at some point further down the line.

Other non-teaching roles in schools

There would appear to be a wider range of non-teaching jobs available in schools than ever before. Many of these roles would be quite suitable for former teachers.

A relatively new role which seems to have appeared in the last decade or so is that of "data manager". This exact job title can vary from school to school but most schools will now employ someone to specifically crunch the school's pupil performance data and help to monitor pupil progress. This member of staff may also take on other administrative roles in the school, such as putting together the school timetable. Job adverts for these kinds of positions usually don't demand particular qualifications and when it comes to experience often all that is usually asked for is experience of using Excel and ideally experience of using a computer system such as SIMS. If you don't have perfect Excel skills, you will find you can brush up quite quickly by taking a short online course. What's more, very few people who haven't worked in schools will have experience of using SIMS and your knowledge of this and the demands of the teaching profession can only be an advantage when competing against applicants with no background in teaching. Salaries often start low but with experience it is not unheard of for them to rise as high as that of a main scale teacher. Of course, you could be put off a job like this for philosophical reasons. If one of the things you dislike about teaching is the constant obsession with data then such a job could be soul destroying. Also, your day to day life will be *very* different from the day to day life of a teacher. This could be a relatively solitary job with a lot of time spent alone in front of a screen.

One of the better paying non-teaching jobs in schools is that of school business manager or bursar. This job would involve handling the school's finances as well as overseeing things such as catering arrangements and the letting of school premises to third parties. There could be a barrier to entry here in that usually these jobs require some background in finance. However, I have seen some jobs advertised where this is not a pre-requisite and there are also qualifications which one can study for in order to prepare for this very unique role. Anglia Ruskin University offers a programme specifically for aspiring school business managers which could help you get an insight in to this unique field, although there is no guarantee of a job at the end of it. Lower level finance assistant jobs in schools often require less experience but are also much lower paid.

If you feel like one of your strengths in the classroom is behaviour management, you may be able to find a pastoral non-teaching job in a school. Many schools advertise for positions such as truancy officer and behaviour support assistant. In some schools, the roles of head of year or designated safeguarding lead can be full time, non-teaching positions. There are also a wide range of administrative jobs available in schools. Jobs working on reception can be highly enjoyable but, as with teaching assistant jobs, there is the issue of low pay. Some slightly more complex administrative roles such as examinations officer will pay a little better, and your experience as an ex-teacher would be highly valued in such a role. If your subject specialism is in ICT or science, you may be able to find a role in a school as a technician.

When it comes to finding a role in a school, I find that the best place to start your search is the Times Educational Supplement website. You no doubt already have experience of using this to find teaching posts. When it comes to non-teaching roles, often it's best to browse rather than search for specific job titles. The best approach is to enter a post code and radius and then leave the search field blank so that the website shows *all* job vacancies within a certain area. You may just stumble across an interesting role which you didn't even know existed.

Jobs in further and higher education

Ex-teachers may be able to find a rewarding role in either a local college or university. Chances are you will be able to draw up a list of all of the colleges and universities which are within commuting distance of where you live. You can then visit the websites of these colleges and universities one by one and see what jobs they have on offer. When it comes to administrative roles in these kinds of institutions, the salaries on offer are typically slightly higher than those on offer in primary or secondary schools although you may not get quite as much holiday.

If you've been reading this book and wondering which new job I have moved into myself, the answer lies here. I now work in a university and market the university by visiting local schools and sixth form colleges. I also collaborate with university students and help them to get involved in the process too. Most universities do this kind of "outreach" work and they will often be keen to recruit those with teaching experience to do it. Sometimes this kind of work also comes under a "widening participation" banner and there is a particular emphasis on engaging with those communities who do not have a strong tradition of progression to higher education. Universities can be wonderful places to work and offer some of the same perks as schools such as good pensions and better than average holidays. You can also benefit from use of the university's facilities such as libraries and sports centres.

Another career option in universities lies in taking on the role of a teacher educator. I must stress that if you are considering this role, you really ought to be someone who has really flourished as a teacher. This is a role for someone who has a keen interest in the world of school education alongside an interest in the academic literature surrounding their subject and how to teach it best. If you enjoy looking through academic journals and research papers but also enjoy spending time in schools too, this could be a job to consider. If you've had positive experiences mentoring and coaching students and NQTs in your career so far, this could all go in your favour, but personally I did not see any teacher educator jobs advertised during my own job search and you might have to be both very patient and willing to travel if you wish to secure one.

Adult education

There are jobs available in further education colleges, community centres and even prisons involving teaching classes to adult learners. There are hundreds of thousands of adults in this country who are either illiterate or innumerate. This acts as both a barrier to success in the workplace and the ability to carry out routine tasks in day to day life. Delivering literacy or numeracy classes to adults who struggle with these things is as task which may be well suited to former teachers, especially those who have a background in English or mathematics. Pay is typically lower than that of a classroom teacher although since some applicants to these positions may not be graduates and will have simply taken a diploma instead, having a degree and QTS could give you a huge advantage. You could still enjoy the challenge of developing your own resources and devising your own lessons, but without a lot of the bureaucracy associated with working in schools.

Educational businesses

Schools have big budgets and there is a diverse array of different companies out there who are trying to get their own slice of that pie. There are a plethora of different companies out there who are trying to offer their services to schools in one way or another in exchange for cash. Some publish textbooks, some run interactive subscription websites, some offer staff CPD during inset days, some sell interactive whiteboards, and so on.

Businesses like this may welcome interest from ex-teachers, especially those ones who have an interest in moving in to more of a sales or marketing role. The key to success here is to identify which companies like this are operating in the area you live in and then find out if any of them may be able to offer you a suitable role. It's no good deciding that you've got your heart set on working for an educational publishing company if there are in fact no educational publishing companies in the city in which you live, which quite frankly is a distinct possibility. If you've worked in schools for many years you may well know already some of the private companies which offer their services to schools. Google a few of them and see if any of them are based near you, you might just strike lucky. If you can find out about any nearby educational conferences (sometimes these can be held in universities), festivals (such as the annual Times Festival of Education) or trade fairs then get yourself along and do some networking!

If you think you have the next big idea which could take the educational world by storm, then who knows maybe you could start your own educational business? Starting any business is a big risk and you always have to accept that your business could well fail. You most likely will want to be in a situation where you have at least one secure stream of income coming from somewhere else before you take a chance on your own self-employment. I am no expert on business, and if you're not either then I suggest you have a long chat with someone who is before you start taking chances. A half-way-house for those who are feeling enterprising but aren't quite brave enough to start a business from scratch would be to look for a franchise opportunity. Many after school tutoring centres such as Kumon and Kip McGrath are franchises. You could apply to start up one of these centres yourself as a franchisee. You will need to stump up some money up front as an investment, most likely thousands of pounds. Being part of a larger chain will make the marketing of your centre a little easier. There's no guarantee of success but if you do succeed then you will enjoy a share of the profits.

Working full time as a self-employed private tutor is uncommon although not unheard of. For more on private tutoring, refer back to the section on money saving and making tips.

As well as educational businesses, there could also be some educational charities operating in your area too. Charities don't only take on volunteers and sometimes the pay can be better than you might think. Take a look at jobs.thirdsector.co.uk and you can search for opportunities in the charity sector.

Councils, academies and the civil service

As more and more schools convert and become academies, the role that local councils are playing in education is now diminishing. However, we are still a long way off complete academisation and councils still employ a variety of staff who play a role in administering school services. As with colleges and universities, there will only be so many councils within commuting distance so keep an eye on the websites of each one for any jobs which might interest you.

Many schools now are not just academies but they are also part of academy chains. Find out which academy chains tend to operate near you and find their websites, there could be career opportunities available there.

A useful website for searching for jobs in the public sector is the civil service jobs website (civilservicejobs.service.gov.uk). Opportunities will vary by region, but you could find job adverts here for organisations like the Department for Education or even Ofsted. If you do end up taking a job with Ofsted, I would walk to school on your last day of teaching. If you don't, there's every chance your colleagues will let your tyres down…

7. Selling Your Skills in Applications

If you've decided that you are going to leave your teaching job, you may be at the stage where you're starting to put together job applications. This chapter will give you tips to help you through the application process. The most important part of that process will be describing the skills you have which make you a suitable candidate for the job. You've got to think about how you can take the myriad of skills which you will have developed whilst teaching and transfer these skills to a new setting. The good news is that teachers use a *huge* range of different skills to do their jobs effectively so you have an awful lot to draw upon. This chapter will start with some general application tips before moving on to describe each of the key skills you have developed in the classroom. Make sure you aren't selling yourself short – you need to describe as many of your skills as you can (and give as much evidence as you can) to give yourself the best chance of success.

General application tips

First of all, make sure you are only applying for jobs which are suitable. All job adverts will list the skills and experience which are required for the job. Employers may also break it down a little and specify things which are *essential* and things which are *desirable*. If you can't meet all the essential skills, you could be wasting your time in applying. With applications, it may well be best to aim for quality and not quantity. It's no good rushing out a load of weak applications for jobs you aren't especially well qualified for. You'd be a lot better of narrowing your focus and completing fewer applications but completing them well.

Accept that completing applications often takes time. Don't be surprised if some applications take you several hours and have to be completed in more than one sitting. Many parts of application forms and processes are self-explanatory. However one of the questions which some leaving teachers may struggle with is the "reason for leaving current job" box. What if the reason is that you have simply grown to hate your job and can't stand it any longer? In situations like this, it's best to spin it around and say what it is that you expect to like about your new job as opposed to what it is that you dislike about your existing role. Your reason then is that whilst you've always enjoyed your current job, you've always had a passion for X and have always secretly wanted to work in that industry. Of course, employers will often be able to read between the lines. That's OK. Any sensible person understands that sometimes people grow dissatisfied with their job and want to change. At the end of the day, if an employer thinks that you have the skills to do the job well then why wouldn't they hire you? They will consider the teaching profession's loss as their gain.

When it comes to referees, your headteacher and line manager are probably your best bet. Everyone, including those outside of education, knows what a headteacher is and they get that they're your boss. They will most likely be expecting the head to be nominated in the references section. Of course, always ask permission before nominating (more on this later).

By far the most important part of the application is the part where you justify why you are suitable for the job. The best way to do this is to work through each of the essential skills specified in the advert in turn and give evidence, using concrete examples, that you have each of these skills. This could also take the form of providing a covering letter containing your justification. But what exactly are the skills you have developed as a teacher, and what examples can you give? Here are what I consider to be some of the main skills you will have developed in your teaching role.

Communication skills

Teaching is all about communication. You will of course be able to cite as examples the hundreds if not thousands of lessons you will have taught over your time in the classroom as instances in which you communicated effectively.

But remember it is not just one but *three* key audiences you communicate with regularly as a teacher – pupils, colleagues and parents. This means that you have the ability not just to communicate effectively but also the ability to tailor your communication to the demands of the particular audience. Even within one audience, such as pupils, you are able to differentiate your approach for different kinds of pupils, taking in to account factors such as their age, ability level and whether they have any special educational needs. Communication with colleagues and parents also involves a high degree of professionalism. You have to be tactful, especially when dealing with sensitive information relating to pupil progress and welfare. To some extent, when you're a teacher the parents are the school's customers. Teaching has parallels to customer facing roles as often you have to deal with queries and feedback from parents in the same way that those working in the customer service industry have to speak to their clients. The dialogue always must remain tactful and courteous.

The communication in teaching often involves explaining difficult concepts to an audience which doesn't necessarily immediately understand them. This involves a degree of patience. Of course, one is explaining new concepts to pupils all of the time in lessons but one must also explain thing to parents too, for example the nature of the curriculum and assessment systems. In teaching, it is not just your audience which keeps changing but also your mode of communication. Teaching involves face to face communication every day with pupils and colleagues. Remember as well that every lesson you teach (and especially every assembly you deliver) is evidence of your public speaking ability. Parents have to be communicated with in a face to face manner at parents' evenings. However you know doubt also communicate effectively in writing too, for example in emails to colleagues and written reports about pupils which are sent home to parents. When it comes to effective communication, you really do have a gold mine of possible examples to plunder.

ICT skills

I see very few jobs advertised nowadays which don't demand excellent ICT skills. Especially in high demand is the ability to use Microsoft Office effectively. Fortunately, effective use of ICT is no sweat for the ex-teacher.

You no doubt will have plenty of experience using just about the entire office suite of programs. You most likely will have designed your own resources and worksheets, perhaps on Microsoft Word or Microsoft Publisher. Maybe you have even published these online? What with the current obsession in schools with pupil data, there's a fair chance you've done a lot of number crunching on Microsoft Excel over the past few years. I'd be amazed if you're not a whizz in making PowerPoint presentations and let's face it the average teacher spends a great deal of their time nowadays glued to Microsoft Outlook sifting their way through dozens of daily emails.

You may also have experience of using software that others outside of teaching are less familiar with. Very few people outside of schools will have experience of using SIMS (or similar software), so if an education related employer is requesting familiarity with this particular piece of software then you're in luck. You might be skilled in using software related to the use of interactive whiteboards such as ActivInspire and Smart Notebook. There are few jobs other than teaching which will require the use of these but you have nonetheless demonstrated here that you have the ability to take a piece of software which once you had no idea how to use and learn very quickly how to master its effective use. This is a skill you can apply elsewhere.

Ability to manage workload

This is a phrase which pops up time after time in job adverts. Sometimes it also may be phrased as something like "the ability to deal with competing priorities all at once". If there's one thing teachers are supremely skilled at, it's this!

Teaching is all about juggling, and boy do you have a lot of balls in the air at once! At any given time chances are you've got lessons to plan, books to mark, emails to reply to, parents to phone, data to enter and did I mention teaching lessons? If this skill is mentioned in a job description, count yourself lucky. You've got this one down. For teachers this ability to multi-task often is second nature, especially if you've been teaching for a while. But how do you put this ability in to words?

The point you need to make is that when faced with several different tasks at once, one has to both be able to prioritise certain tasks and deprioritise others. The tasks that get prioritised are the ones where there is an impending deadline. If parents' evening is this evening, you'd better have all your data printed out by the time it starts. But what about the tasks which are deprioritised? Well whilst deprioritising is often perfectly appropriate, one still needs a system in place to make sure that tasks which are deprioritised are nonetheless eventually completed. A simple systems using lists, diaries or computer software usually does the trick here. Teachers also have to manage their workload not just in the short term but in the longer term too. You have to juggle the tasks you face within any given week but at the same time you have to realise that certain times of the year (e.g. exam season) are much more busy than others (e.g. August). Therefore teachers exercise a degree of foresight in thinking about how tasks should be prioritised across a whole year, not just across weeks or days.

Working with young people

If you're applying for a non-teaching job where you'll still be working with young people and one of the skills required is to work with young people successfully, then again you are in luck.

There are few if any professionals who have more experience of working with young people than teachers. If many of the applicants you're competing against are not from a teaching background, you almost certainly will have more relevant experience than them when it comes to working with youngsters. For some applicants, the only experience they may have to draw upon in their applications might be the odd evening spent volunteering at their local scout group, yet you have probably notched up thousands of hours in the company of children and in that time you will have learnt an awful lot about what makes them tick. Rather than assuming that's it's just a given, make sure you sell the experience you have with young people on your application.

After working successfully as a teacher you have more than just the experience of working with young people. What you have is the ability to communicate effectively with young people as well as the ability to motivate and inspire young people to achieve. These are not easy things to do. It's not easy to get a group of disinterested Year 9 pupils to learn about igneous rock at the end of a rainy Thursday afternoon. If you can do this, you must have excellent people skills and a unique ability to motivate others.

Working with young people in schools also involves having an understanding of crucial child safeguarding issues so don't forget to point this out too. All teachers have had experience of dealing with pastoral issues even if only in their capacity as a form tutor or classroom teacher so don't forget about your ability to deal with those awkward moments whether it's relating to bullying, squabbling or anything else. Related to this is the ability to manage young people's behaviour. Many adults, especially parents, may assume that they have the ability to do this in a work environment but as we all know behaviour management is a unique skill which very few people get right first time around. When talking about your behaviour management abilities, try to keep things as positive as possible by focussing on your ability to engage and enthuse young people as opposed to your ability to strike fear in to their hearts!

Other skills

These skills don't necessarily warrant their own section, but here are five more skills which you should be quick to mention on applications:

Teamwork: Some employers with little knowledge of teaching may assume that teaching is a solitary profession where one stays alone in one's classroom all day and works completely independently. Be quick to point out that team work is essential, especially in the case of collaborating with departmental colleagues in coming up with new ideas and developing new schemes of work and resources.

Organisational skills: Organised a few school trips recently? Don't forget to mention it. There are an awful lot of steps to be taken in organising a successful event, especially when other people's children are involved. Organising your lessons, the curriculum and your huge collection of teaching resources is no mean feat either.

Creativity: Some people who don't teach don't realise that teachers have to devise their lessons themselves. They just think teachers turn up and work their way through lessons which have already been prepared for them by the school, or even the Government! Point out how untrue this is and make clear the degree of creativity which is required to teach successfully. Teachers have to be creative not just before lessons but during lessons too. When things don't go to plan, teachers deploy their ability to think on their feet.

Professionalism: Take advantage of the fact that you are leaving a *profession* and that professional conduct is required at all times. This encompasses a multitude of things ranging from the way one dresses to the way one behaves outside of school on social media.

Management skills: The extent of your people management skills will depend on the particular path you have trodden in your teaching career. If you've been a head of department or even assistant head then you can give some quite explicit examples of people management. Even if you haven't, perhaps you could refer to time you have helped to coach new or student teachers? If all else fails, you can always refer to your behaviour management abilities.

Interviews

This is not a book about interview technique, and a quick Google search can provide you with more interview technique tips than you could care to read. However, if you have been offered an interview then there are two things I would say. First of all – congratulations! Even if you are unsuccessful, you now know that you have the ability to impress an employer enough to get shortlisted. Secondly, remind yourself that you have been successful at teaching interviews in the past. As someone who has been interviewed for both teaching jobs and non-teaching jobs, I can tell you that teaching interviews tend to be tougher.

Why are teaching interviews tougher? Mainly because usually you have to teach a lesson as well as do the actual interview. There are two big things to prepare for, two things to get nervous about and potentially two things which could go wrong. It can be quite refreshing to have an interview experience which is just that – there is simply an interview and that's it. All of your preparation time can be spent doing that all important homework researching the organisation and you won't have to spend half of your preparation time photocopying and cutting up a card sort task. As teachers, many of us will in fact be extremely adept at dealing with stress. I remember attending an interview and speaking with one of the other candidates who was not a teacher. She said to me "I was feeling nervous this morning but then I calmed myself down by thinking of today as just another day at work." I didn't say it out loud but I remember thinking to myself – "for me this is actually a hell of a lot less stressful than just another day at work!" If you can handle the stress of teaching, you can handle the stress of an interview. Trust me.

I hope this list of skills has been helpful. You should use this list to first of all help you select the right jobs to apply for in the first place. Once you've done that I hope the list will help you to draw on the relevant experience you have from teaching to explain how you could rise to a new challenge. Remember, you don't have to reinvent the wheel every time you apply for a new job. There is a place for copying and pasting, but don't do it blindly or without thinking.

8. Going Out Gracefully

This chapter concerns not necessarily the process of finding a new job but the process of leaving your old one. During my time in schools I saw all too many teachers leave in somewhat acrimonious circumstances and all too few teachers go out gracefully. You only get one opportunity to leave any given job so make sure you do it right.

Resignation etiquette

The first step in the leaving process is deciding that you're going to leave. When I went through this process I decided to confide in just a couple of trusted colleagues and that was it. You don't want a rumour going around the whole school that you may be leaving especially if you end up not leaving or don't leave for many months or even years. Remember too that rumours in school usually tend to inevitably make it to pupils through the grapevine.

If you're feeling unhappy in school it may be tempting to go and tell your headteacher that you're planning on leaving. You may think that by saying this that the head will panic and will then try and improve your working conditions. You may also think that this allows you in some strange way to get one over on your head. You have to ask yourself: what will I really achieve by such a move? Your head may think you are bluffing and if you end up not leaving after you've said that you will you end up looking weak. Your head might even chose to call your bluff and start to put you through a competency procedure whilst starting to look for your replacement.

In my opinion, the best thing to do is to wait until you have found at least one job that you are genuinely planning on applying for. Once you've done that, and remember that finding the right job could take several months, approach your head, explain your intentions and ask if they are happy to be nominated as a referee on your application. This way, you are approaching the situation from a position of strength. Make it clear to your head that you might not be successful and that you might change your mind. Reassure them that so long as you are working at the school they will always be able to expect 100% from you. I hope you'll find that most heads are understanding and supportive. During your conversation, ask if your head is happy to act as a referee again should your application be unsuccessful. This saves you from having to have this conversation all over again in future. Also, it isn't unreasonable for you to ask the head to keep your intentions reasonably quiet for the time being. If your head seems to want you to stay and tries to offer you some sort of adjustment to make your work life easier, think this over very carefully and don't rush in to any decisions.

Throughout the course of any conversations with your head, always keep in the back of your mind that they will be writing your reference!

Resignation dates

The gospel when it comes to your possible resignation dates is your contract, so dig this out if possible. If you're working in a state school, I suspect you'll find that there are only three dates in the year on which you may leave. These are 30th April, 31st August and 31st December. To leave in April, you'll need to get your notice in by 28th/29th February, to leave in August you'll need to get your notice in by 31st May and to leave in December notice will be required by 31st October.

These rules can be annoyingly inflexible, and it means that teachers need to give an awful lot more notice than most other workers. Because of these restrictions, some teachers chose to transition by first moving in to a more flexible role, for example supply teaching. Then they can look for other jobs and leave at the drop of a hat when they find one. Personally, I chose to stick it out and cross that bridge when I came to it.

Remember, the rules don't mean that you have to give that much notice necessarily, they just mean that if you don't give the required notice then in theory the headteacher can force you to stay until the next appropriate resignation date. If you do a disappearing act, you will be in breach of your contract. In theory, you could be taken to court for this. In practice, that won't happen but you will have burnt your bridges, left your job on a rather sour note and potentially caused some serious disruption to children's education.

If I were you, I wouldn't let these dates disrupt your job searching process. If you want to leave, then look for new jobs all year round. If the worst comes to the worst and you are offered a job which you then can't take because of dates, then so be it. At least you will get a confidence boost as you will now know that there are other jobs out there. In practice, you will often find that your head has common sense and will allow you to leave early anyway. What kind of head would force someone to stay against their will? Once a head knows that a teacher has had enough and is ready to go, it's usually in the interests of all parties concerned (the teacher, the school and its pupils) to say farewell. Teachers forced to stay are likely to put in the bare minimum of effort, leave every day at 3.30p.m. and refuse to do any task unless they are contractually obliged to. No school wants staff who act like that.

Resignation letters

When that happy moment comes when you've been offered a new job and accepted it, it's time to seal the deal by putting your resignation in writing. There's no reason why this letter can't be short, sweet and to the point. For example...

Your address

Their address

Monday 23rd May 2016

Dear Mr Skinner,

I am writing to inform you that I shall be resigning from my post. My last day of employment with Springfield Elementary School will be Wednesday 31st August 2016.

I would like to thank you for the opportunity with which you have provided me over the course of the last ten years. I wish Springfield Elementary School best wishes for the future.

Yours sincerely,

Edna Krabappel

Job done! Make sure you give the correct resignation date. For example, if you're leaving at the end of the school year then don't give a resignation date as 31st July as you then may not get paid for August. If you think your resignation letter is also the place to share a piece of your mind, then read on…

Don't burn your bridges

If things have gotten a little bit ugly towards the end of your teaching career, then you might be tempted upon your departure to tell other colleagues, managers or your headteacher a few home truths. If you're thinking of doing this, _please don't!_

I'll tell you exactly why. If you do decide to give colleagues a piece of your mind, you could live to regret it. Ah yes, you say, but isn't it also true that I could in a few months' time regret _not_ telling them exactly what I thought of them? Very true, but should this happen you could always put pen to paper (or fingers to keyboard) and write to them and them what you think. But chances are you won't, because a few months down the line you'll realise that leaving gracefully was in fact the right thing to do rather that souring the memory of what could have been a very lengthy and significant period of your life. On the other hand, once things _are_ said there is no going back. They're out there for good and you can't take them back.

Behaving appropriately at the end of your career is important for both moral and practical reasons. As unhappy as you might be, it is always possible that you could end up going back to teaching. Even if you don't end up working at the same school or for the same headteacher, word of any unprofessional behaviour can soon spread. When you leave a school I think that you should try to remain as humble as possible. I've seen colleagues leave school with the attitude that somehow they are irreplaceable and their department, or even school will crumble without them. It never does. People are replaced, and life goes on.

9. Case Studies

This chapter features five real case studies of teachers who have made their escape and moved on to pastures new. Each of the five stories is unique, and I hope that this will help you to see that there is an almost infinite number of different paths to take when leaving the profession.

All the words are spoken by the teachers themselves, although names have been changed to preserve anonymity.

Case study 1 – Lyndon

Why did you decide to leave?

I had become very disillusioned with what was happening in education since 2010. The massive increase in workload, scrutiny and general mistrust in the profession made me decide that I needed to look for something else. A new head at the school seemed determined to get rid of staff she didn't like.

I started looking for a new job around 2013 when I'd paid the mortgage off. I realised that any new job would almost certainly require a drop in income so that made things somewhat easier.

Around that time workload continued to spiral. I tried to tell my colleagues to fight the workload increase through action short of strike action but I was effectively isolated as there was a culture of fear in the school. I was losing sleep, I had a month off with work related stress and an irregular heartbeat.

I complained to the head that the workload was affecting my health and that I wasn't going to do it anymore. I was threatened with misconduct. With union advice that was dropped and I was referred to occupational health but their report was ignored. That was the line in the sand for me.

What job do you do now and how did you find it?
I work as a railway transport planner working for a friend. I look into how more capacity can be found on different routes in different parts of the country. I do the planning, write reports and present reports to clients. I do a bit of travelling but mainly work at home.

Just before the summer holidays a friend who set up his own railway consultancy business rang me up and said he was looking for extra people to work for his small company. I had always been interested in railways, so it came as a real lifeline. I did some work for him over the summer holidays. He seemed impressed and subsequently offered me a six month contract which has been extended indefinitely.

I started work in October having left somewhat suddenly following a disagreement with my headteacher (amazing the freedom you have once you've resigned!). More details can be found on my blog.[17]

I consider myself very fortunate and now earn almost as much as I did as a UPS3 teacher.

What is your best piece of advice for someone who wants to leave?
Make sure that you have the support of your family (I did). Try

also to ensure that you are financially sound although in my case I'd decided that my health was more important.

Ignore all the silly initiatives that are continually being introduced in schools. Do your own thing but be careful if you have an aggressive SLT.

Remember, that it will take time to find something else. You may get a lucky break like I did, but if you are determined then you will eventually get something. If possible, get a bit of experience in your chosen new field of work.

Do you have any regrets about leaving?
No regrets whatsoever. However, I was very annoyed and still am about the manner of my departure (see the blog). I was not allowed to say goodbye to other staff nor the kids. I do miss the kids but I do not miss the stress and pressure that modern teaching entails.

Although I only get a few weeks holiday a year (compared to teaching) I now have more free time, I work hard but am stress free. If I want to take a day off in the week I work one at the weekend instead. As long as the job is done my boss is not bothered. How good is that?

Early September always feels odd. I feel I should be getting stressed about returning to work but I don't have that feeling. My wife is still teaching and I feel I might be getting stressed on her behalf.

I always imagined that once I'd retired / left teaching I would do supply to top up my wages but I now feel that even that is unlikely which is a shame after 30 years' teaching experience.

Case study 2 – James

Why did you decide to leave?

I had to leave as I was summarily forced out. The details are shocking and should be illegal so I've condensed it a lot...

I had taught full time for 19 years straight, it had been my first and only career. I'd had a few minor health blips during this time which were naturally resolving themselves. One of my relatives was also terminally ill during this time and they have since died. Then unluckily for me, the long serving headmaster I had worked with retired on his own health grounds, exhausted.

The older headteacher had, before he left, essentially given the head of department role to a teacher who had never worked anywhere else and who had shockingly narrow people skills. Despite this, and despite getting frozen out of more and more of his self-made cliques, I soldiered on, often being shouted down in meetings, given very hard timetables, overlooked for small promotions in favour of newer younger staff, and so forth.

Finally in 2012 the penny dropped. The new head and newish head of department wanted me out, despite tonnes of experience, because I had dared to get older and have other commitments. I should add that I regularly worked twelve hour days, despite all this stress.

Soon, despite fourteen years of top appraisals, the also newly arrived and notorious performance manager deputy head threatened me with capability. Trumped up charges. There had been a slight dip in GCSE results from four years prior! I involved my union who took school to task. We thought the school had backed off. The head of department continued despite his bullying and my health deteriorated. I collapsed three times at or just before going to work, and had to get my heart restarted. There was not only *no* duty of care whatsoever, I felt that if I didn't go into work they'd fire me, as the head remained intentionally ambiguous about whether I was or was not on capability proceedings and at what stage, formal or informal. Finally things got very bad, two months before planned surgery. Yet I still managed to return to work within a week, after emergency heart surgery! What an utter mug I was! But this insane brainwashed Stockholm syndrome mindset is what can make us our own worst enemies. Two months after that, I got called in and told I was now on formal capability, which would ensure I would never get another job. Only then did I break and get the long overdue union involved. They went for work-related stress leave. I had about a month off but I needed much longer. My phased return was rigged so that it ended the day before term did. If, they warned, I dared come in on the last day of term, formal capability, which the union rep and work-related stress haggling had stalled, would start. My last day in the school was awful. Most of my older colleagues had long gone. Many of the younger ones hated me as they didn't know about my heart and must have assumed I was skiving. They ignored me, and the head of department would have if I hadn't insisted on shaking his little hand before I left. Two friends cowered in the corner and waited for him to leave before running after me. Other students and colleagues who'd known me for years hovered as well, but frankly it was a despicable way to end a long career at what had once been a good school. No leaving speech, no card, no nothing.

What job do you do now and how did you find it?
Some friends and family members tipped me off that there was money to be made in tutoring. I'd always tutored and found it reassuring to skip back into a familiar and always rewarding line of work. I was now only working six hours a day! That was when

I started to heal and get better. I realise now that I'd been mad enough to make myself dangerously ill and only just managed to get away with it. The school gave me a paltry payoff and even quibbled over that.

Private tuition is a growth market and, as schools are heading down the toilet at the rate of knots, it will soon be saturated. It's hard planning your own workload and haggling direct with parents for slots. Some kids and parents forget to turn up, and a few are too demanding, but most are a joy to work with and I realise that either my old school had particularly abysmal parents, managers, and spoilt kids, or that the SLT lied to me about the complaints that had been made against me. Which do you think it was?!

What is your advice for someone who wants to leave?
1) I would leave sooner rather than later. Experience isn't always valued in teaching.
2) Be sure to be in a union. This means you can get useful feedback from a third party if you find yourself in a difficult situation. Always communicate with your union using a personal email address, as it could be possible for staff in school to snoop on work email accounts!
3) Stay especially clear of teaching if you're experiencing health problems.
4) Manage your money and have at least three months' worth of spending in the bank to cushion the financial impact.
5) Always try to jump before being pushed, but research potential new schools carefully first.
6) Teachers are born workaholics, so don't be daunted by retraining! I've been looking at education training, the civil service and local charities.

7) Believe in yourself because nobody else will!

Case study 3 – Stuart

Why did you decide to leave teaching?

I came to primary teaching from academia in the early noughties, training through the GTP program in a junior school which, during my first year, was judged to be outstanding. The school had a number of very established staff in key leadership positions, knew what it was trying to achieve and was excellent at producing evidence without adding workload to its teaching staff. Its only fault from a teaching perspective was a very dry and prescriptive approach to the curriculum, though this was rectified by a new headteacher who came with a strong philosophy and vision for a much more creative curriculum. We made a lot of change while maintaining our end of Year 6 attainment. Over a five year period I joined the leadership team, was seconded to local authority and was on track for headship.

In the aftermath of the recession, both local authority and government began to develop a disrespectful, bullying attitude towards schools and educators which started to influence public attitudes. Disheartened, I moved into the independent sector where I worked as a specialist teacher and subject leader for some years, before being tempted back to a Year 6 leader and teacher role with my previous employer. I quickly discovered that things had moved from disheartening to intolerable in the state sector during my years away.

Most damaging for me was that during this period of absence from the maintained sector, Key Stage 1 testing was replaced with teacher assessment. As a junior school we saw immediate inflation in our students' levels as they entered from our feeder school into Year 3; the inflation was so great that, for us to make the required progress as a high-functioning school, nearly 90% of our students needed to be level 6+ at the end of Year 6. This was clearly impossible to achieve: Ofsted put the school into special measures, I resigned on the spot, the local authority removed the head, forced an amalgamation with the infant school and put the infant school's head (who was the root of our demise) in charge of the new through school. Morale was floored, there were tears daily and the entire staff turned over within 18 months. The whole affair was handled without integrity or competence by Ofsted, the local authority or the very narrow individuals placed into the school the support the journey out of special measures; it cemented my growing perception that an education sector managed by the state was not one in which I could function with integrity. I left and will not return.

What do you do now, and what advice would you give to others?

Following the special measures debacle, I went overseas to teach for a couple of years and have recently returned to a sabbatical year during which I have come to realise that education as it has evolved is no longer for me. I regret neither the time spent on a teaching career nor the decision to leave, and while I am currently unfocused and looking for new inspiration, the journey is exciting and I am looking forward to seeing where it leads. My advice to anyone looking to leave is simply to not allow fear of change to keep you in an unsatisfactory or unhealthy position: be true to yourself and don't rush.

Case study 4 - Charles

Why did you decide to leave?

I resigned voluntarily from my full-time head of subject post in a LEA high school at age 50, at the end of 2009. We had paid off the balance of our mortgage the previous year, and at the time my wife was in full-time employment in another school, so we could afford the financial change. The school was a specialist 'college' and I'd been head of its specialist subject since it had achieved specialist college status. I'd worked there for just over 20 years under various headteachers in a number of roles, and had played a central part in building up the specialist subject from scratch and resourcing it. My main reason for leaving was the arrival of a new headteacher whose personal agenda and dictatorial leadership style made it clear that I didn't share their aspirations for the future of my subject. Fundamental changes were being made with which I disagreed, and goals were being set that I felt were not achievable. Responsibilities that I had held were being handed to those more on-side with the head's thinking. The writing was on the wall, so I paid attention to it and I left of my own volition before they could make up an excuse to push me. I wasn't the only one to take this decision, but many of the others escaped into early retirement whilst I had no other job to go to.

What job do you do now and how did you find it?

I initially opted for supply teaching, so I signed up with the LEA's preferred supply agency. I spent around 18 months working on daily and short term supply assignments in a variety of local schools, averaging 0.6 full time equivalent, with a reasonable amount of the work paid to scale (i.e. pensionable). I was fortunate in that I had experience of a range of GCSE subjects, including ICT, which has always been a shortage subject. Schools were definitely grateful for having a supply who knew one end of a computer from another. I started getting longer term contracts in certain schools, 6, 10, and 12 months respectively, all at 0.6 full time equivalent. Most of this work was pensionable.

During my last year as a teacher (2012-13) I took on a part-time seasonal job as a museum guide with the local council, between April and September. This fitted in with my teaching commitments and drew on my existing skills as an educator. The location is idyllic and the site (a rural working museum) is run single handed so I was well-prepared by supply teaching for an independent role. My final 12 month teaching contract was due to be renewed by the headteacher, but I declined. Whilst the school was very good, the department that I had been working in was not a happy one, with high staff turnover, out of date subject content and minimal leadership due to an impending retirement. I felt completely unprepared for what was promising to be an Ofsted year, so I chose not to seek renewal of the contract, and decided to leave the classroom at age 54 in August 2013.

Having spent some time earlier in my teaching career trading in collectables as a sideline, I decided to revive this as an income source. During summer 2013 I began visiting my local auction house and started buying up house clearance lots for resale on the collector's market, both at fairs and online through eBay. This enterprise continues to this day, and fits in nicely with my other jobs as it is flexible - I can do as much or as little of it as I need. I have extended my range to include buying items at continental flea markets when on holiday, and from local car boot sales, but my main source of stock is auctions. I have gained a new skill set and knowledge base in order to research, recognise, repair and restore the items that I trade in. It has been something of an education for me to put it mildly, and it's great fun too.

My other job is a joint enterprise with my wife, who set herself up as an independent education consultant during 2010. We identified a new 'niche' in a particular area of the 2014 KS2 National Curriculum, and decided to address it by offering freelance half day subject workshops in Primary Schools to assist pupils' understanding of the subject matter. This has become quite successful, we travel around the region, and other opportunities have arisen from it. We thoroughly enjoy it - being able to enter a classroom on our own terms and engage pupils in a manner of our choice whilst being unhampered by excessive paperwork has become an increasingly rare commodity in teaching these days.

What is your best piece of advice for someone who wants to leave?

First and foremost pay no attention whatsoever to the old "those who can, do.." adage that implies teachers are useless in non-teaching roles. It is utter rubbish and always has been. Have faith in your skills, knowledge, persistence, endurance and personal qualities and think carefully about how you can apply them elsewhere. Secondly, don't look down on commercial activity as being somehow grubby without trying it - people are happy to pay money for the things they want, and it's perfectly acceptable for you to sell them those things ethically in order to make a living. As a natural communicator who can deal with all sorts of people you may actually be quite good at it, so be prepared to give it a go. Thirdly, there are ways of educating people outside Ofsted's hamster wheel - it is still possible to teach without pointless box ticking. Give careful thought to how you might do this if teaching is a vocation for you. Finally, if you've had enough of being ordered around by others, especially the know nothing greasy pole climbers, opt for self-employment - then the only idiotic management decisions you'll ever have to deal with be your own!

Do you have any regrets about leaving?

Leaving full-time teaching? Only one. My headteacher deliberately prevented me from making a proper leaving speech to my colleagues on the day I left the school that I'd worked in for over two decades. The head wrongly believed I was going to do a Geoffrey Howe, when all I'd wanted to do was say a heartfelt public 'thank you' to the people who'd really mattered to me. I regret that missed opportunity, and will never forgive the head for denying it to me. Given the level of petty spite involved on their part it's easy to understand why I have no other regrets about leaving that particular school.

Leaving formal teaching four years later? My only regret is that I feel I let down a perfectly civilised and respected headteacher by not seeking to renew a contract that he was happy to see renewed. However it was 12 months only, I saw it through to the end, and I'd notified him of my decision early in the school year - temporary contracts can work both ways can't they?

In other respects I haven't yet left - I still educate people about the past through the museum, and I still work in the classroom with my wife running subject workshops. The difference is it's on my terms, using my professional experience and judgment once more, and it's not beset on all sides by the tyranny of statistics and pointless paperwork. I have no regrets about that whatsoever.

Conclusion

No job is perfect. Some are badly paid and many are stressful. Some jobs are boring and don't provide enough challenge. Many involve long hours. Sometimes, there is a constant tension between workers and their managers which is corrosive. On other occasions, we can't quite put our finger on what's wrong with our job but we know deep down that it's not for us.

Most of us spend almost half of our waking lives at work. Finding the right career then is surely something of crucial importance. Whilst we can't be unrealistic in our expectations and expect every single day to be an extravaganza of fun, when we realise that we are unhappy more often than we are happy then it's probably time to move on.

Schools are becoming increasingly difficult places to work. We might point the finger of blame at ministers, governments, regulators such as Ofsted or even headteachers. But in doing so we should remember that these people and institutions don't necessarily have bad intentions. They are thinking about the education of children, and they want to make sure that children have the best education possible. This is admirable, but it is irresponsible for these people and institutions not to think about the effect that their actions may be having on teachers.

As teachers we care about children. For me, the purpose of education is to successfully prepare children for a prosperous and happy adulthood. So if as teachers then we care about adult happiness, why do we often pay so little attention to our own? It can be soul destroying to spend one's career helping others to lead a successful and happy life whilst knowing in the back of one's mind that the stresses of one's job means that such happiness is never likely to be available to oneself.

Whilst we must avoid seeing a career change as some sort of panacea which will solve all of life's problems, I believe it is irrational to continue in a job feeling dissatisfied if there are more gratifying career opportunities available elsewhere. When the spark is gone, we owe it to not just ourselves but also to the children we teach to move on. I hope that this book has helped you to make a rational choice about your future career.

As I now look at my watch, I'm conscious of the fact that we don't have long left and the bell is just about to ring. But before I ask you to pack away and stand behind your chairs, make sure you have written down today's homework in your homework diaries. Today's homework is to assess your current career situation with brutal honesty and to strive from today onwards to make the changes which you believe necessary to rebalance your life and to achieve less stress, greater satisfaction and greater happiness. I must warn you that I have a zero tolerance policy when it comes to homework completion and I will not be accepting any excuses from you. Although I may not be teaching this particular class again, at the very least I expect you to email me and share your story with me.

Good luck! Class dismissed.

facebook.com/schoolsoutphilfletcher
contact.schoolsout.book@gmail.com

References

1. *School Teachers' Review Body Twenty-Fifth Report* (2015)
   https://www.gov.uk/government/uploads/system/uploads
   /attachment_data/file/412795/47520_School_Teachers_Revi
   ew_Body_Accessible.pdf
2. *Teachers' workload diary survey 2013*
   https://www.gov.uk/government/publications/teachers-
   workload-diary-survey-2013
3. *Who, What, Why: What do Tube drivers do and how much do
   they earn?* BBC News (2015)
   http://www.bbc.co.uk/news/magazine-33459515
4. Nearly half of England's teachers plan to leave in next five
   years, *The Guardian* (2016)
   https://www.theguardian.com/education/2016/mar/22/teac
   hers-plan-leave-five-years-survey-workload-england
5. *School workforce in England: November 2015*
   https://www.gov.uk/government/statistics/school-
   workforce-in-england-november-2015
6. https://getintoteaching.education.gov.uk/explore-my-
   options/return-to-teaching
7. Old, Andrew (2013) *Some Quick Tips for NQTs and Trainees*
   https://teachingbattleground.wordpress.com/2013/09/03/so
   me-quick-tips-for-nqts/
8. Worth, J., Bamford, S. and Durbin, B. (2015) *Should I Stay or
   Should I Go? NFER Analysis of Teachers Joining and Leaving*

the Profession
https://www.nfer.ac.uk/publications/LFSA01/LFSA01.pdf

9. https://getintoteaching.education.gov.uk/funding-and-salary/teacher-salaries

10. Office for National Statistics *Annual Survey of Hours and Earnings: 2014 Provisional Results*
http://www.ons.gov.uk/employmentandlabourmarket/peopleinwork/earningsandworkinghours/bulletins/annualsurveyofhoursandearnings/2014-11-19

11. https://www.agr.org.uk/Press-Releases/agr-summer-survey-graduate-job-vacancies-predicted-to-rise-by-17-#.V8V_xqJzMz4

12. Pearson (2015) *Why Teach?*
http://whyteach.lkmco.org/wp-content/uploads/2015/10/Embargoed-until-Friday-23-October-2015-Why-Teach.pdf

13. https://www.teachers.org.uk/edufacts/workload

14. Office for National Statistics *Annual Survey of Hours and Earnings: 2015 Provisional Results*
http://www.ons.gov.uk/employmentandlabourmarket/peopleinwork/earningsandworkinghours/bulletins/annualsurveyofhoursandearnings/2015provisionalresults

15. BBC News (2016) *Warning over England's 'teacher brain drain'*
http://www.bbc.co.uk/news/education-35660457

16. BBC News (2016) *Why teachers quit the UK to work abroad*
http://www.bbc.co.uk/news/education-35666644

17. https://exscienceteacherblog.wordpress.com/

Printed in Great Britain
by Amazon

77454739R00071